Critical Corporate Communications

Critical Corporate Communications

A Best Practice Blueprint

NAOMI LANGFORD-WOOD
& BRIAN SALTER

JOHN WILEY & SONS, LTD

This publication is designed to provide accurate and authoritative information in regard to
the subject matter covered. It is sold on the understanding that the Publisher is not engaged
in rendering professional services. If professional advice or other expert assistance is
required, the services of a competent professional should be sought.

Other Wiley Editorial Offices

John Wiley & Sons Inc., 111 River Street, Hoboken, NJ 07030, USA

Jossey-Bass, 989 Market Street, San Francisco, CA 94103-1741, USA

Wiley-VCH Verlag GmbH, Boschstr. 12, D-69469 Weinheim, Germany

John Wiley & Sons Australia Ltd, 33 Park Road, Milton, Queensland 4064, Australia

John Wiley & Sons (Asia) Pte Ltd, 2 Clementi Loop #02-01, Jin Xing Distripark, Singapore
129809

John Wiley & Sons Canada Ltd, 22 Worcester Road, Etobicoke, Ontario, Canada M9W 1L1

British Library Cataloguing in Publication Data

A catalogue record for this book is available from the British Library

ISBN 0-470-84763-8

Typeset in 11/15.5 pt ITC Garamond Light by Footnote Graphics, Warminster, Wiltshire.
Printed and bound in Great Britain by Biddles Ltd, Guildford and King's Lynn.
This book is printed on acid-free paper responsibly manufactured from sustainable forestry
in which at least two trees are planted for each one used for paper production.

Contents

Series Foreword

Iam delighted to be able to introduce to you the *CBI Fast Track Series*. The book you are holding is the outcome of a significant new publishing partnership between the CBI and John Wiley & Sons (Wiley). It is one of the first in a long line of high quality materials on which the CBI and Wiley will collaborate. Before saying a little about this partnership, I would like to briefly introduce you to the CBI.

With a direct corporate membership employing over 4 million and a trade association membership representing over 6 million of the workforce, the CBI is the premier organisation speaking for companies in the UK. We represent, directly and indirectly, over 200 000 companies employing more than 40% of UK private sector workforce. The majority of blue-chip organisations and industry leaders from the FTSE 250 are members, as well as a significant number of small to medium sized companies (SMEs).* Our mission is to ensure that the government of the day, Whitehall, Brussels and the wider community understand the needs of British business. The CBI takes an active role in forming policies that enable UK companies to compete and prosper, and we ensure that the lines of communication between private and public leaders are always open on a national scale as well as via our regional networks.

The appropriateness of a link between the CBI and a leading business publisher like Wiley cannot be understated. Both organisations have a vested interest in efficiently and effectively serving the needs of businesses of all sizes. Both are forward-thinkers; constantly trend-spotting to envision where the next issues and concerns lie. Both maintain a global outlook in servicing the needs of their local customers. And finally, both champion the adoption of best practice among the groups they represent.

* Foreign companies that maintain registered offices in the UK are also eligible for CBI membership.

Which brings us back to this series. Each *CBI Fast Track* book offers a complete best practice briefing in a selected topic, along with a blueprint for successful implementation. The aim is to help enterprises achieve peak performance across key disciplines. The series will continue to evolve as new and different issues force their way to the top of the corporate agenda.

I do hope you enjoy this book and would encourage you to look out for further titles from the CBI and Wiley. Here's to all the opportunities the future holds and to *Fast Track* success with your own corporate agenda.

Digby Jones
Director-General, CBI

About the Authors

Naomi Langford-Wood and Brian Salter are twenty-first-century business experts, practical visionaries and serial entrepreneurs. Coming from very different backgrounds, they are specialists in all aspects of communication and realistic business usage of new technologies, and the development of powerful business and marketing strategies.

A serial entrepreneur, businesswoman, writer and speaker over the past 20 years, Naomi's career has encompassed 14 directorships. Having worked in a variety of blue chip companies, she went on to set up several new businesses including a software house, public relations agencies and consultancies.

Brian was for many years a presenter, writer and producer of business, current affairs and feature programmes on the BBC's World Service and BBC Radio 4. He has subsequently directed communications divisions in household-name companies.

Because of these core skills, their company – Topspin™ Group (www.topspin-group.com) – has increasingly found itself in demand for high level advice on the use of communication and emerging technologies within business and – in the process – recognised that the cornerstone requirement is often to conduct a company communications audit, as a prerequisite to creating effective market positioning and customer-focused strategies for the client.

Acknowledgements

We would like to thank the many people who helped us in the writing of this book. In particular:

Iain Burns, General Manager of Corporate Communications at British Airways

Marybelle Gander at Foursquare Productions

Carol Jones, Principal of Select Speakers Ltd

Nicholas Slater, Barrister specialising in European law

Ian Takats, Group IS Director within the Health and Fitness industry

Dianne Thompson, CEO of Camelot plc

Keith Turner, Senior Partner of Turner Coulston, Solicitors

Chris Tyrrell, CEO of Tyrrell Automotive Ltd

Peter Waine, CEO of Hanson Green Ltd

Andrew West, Managing Partner of West Associates

Roger White, Director of Corporate Affairs at Pricewaterhouse-Coopers plc

Introduction

In 2001, when the green light was finally given to BAA plc for the building of the new Terminal 5 at Heathrow Airport, it had followed a full 13 years of political lobbying, press relations, public relations, customer relations, investor relations and any other relations you could care to mention to achieve the decision seen as crucial by the airports operator. The then-MD of Heathrow Airport Ltd, Alan Proctor, had even set up a team in his Public Affairs division way back in 1988 to start planning the whole communications exercise, knowing that to get the go-ahead for such a massive project could, on past record, take well over a decade to achieve.

Yet when Christopher Tyrrell set up Tyrrell Automotive in a tiny business park on the outskirts of Buckingham in 1999, how did it manage to attain almost instant success with no advertising, no paid-for public relations work and no press contacts, while relying almost solely on the merits of a website to promote its services, from which all its business flowed?

No business is an island and, without exception, communication lies at the heart of every successful – and unsuccessful – business. It's obvious that any business needs to communicate with everyone who has anything to do with it. But what, how, why, when and with whom are the key questions to be asked with every form of communication.

We'll be starting out in this book with that last question: With whom? All organisations need to communicate with a number of different audiences, and sometimes what they say to one will not necessarily be the same as what they wish to say to another. Likewise what feedback they solicit from one may not be what they solicit or receive from another. External audiences, for instance, may be given a slightly glossier picture of the fortunes of a company than those within the organisation. There will almost certainly be those, too, who will need to be 'in the know' with regard to any bad news or commercially sensitive information, and so getting to know your audiences has to be a key consideration in any business. There is a very fine dividing line between showing something in a good light and giving misleading information.

Just as important as identifying the key audiences that you wish to reach and communicate with is knowing what it is you want to communicate and why you are trying to say it in the first place. Surely that's obvious, isn't it? Well, no, it isn't. It is quite surprising how many organisations 'open their mouths before putting their brains into gear'. So we will also be looking in this book at some of the things you may wish to be communicating with your audiences since communications can really be viewed only in a holistic way, otherwise one could argue that the whole exercise has been a waste of time.

Finally, knowing what it is you want to communicate is only half the story. Nowadays there is a veritable plethora of communication channels available, some of which are good in some situations but hopeless in others. So we will also be concentrating on the means whereby the flow of information can be effected.

It is an unfortunate fact that something that most people tend to take for granted so often ends up as a confused set of ideas. When disaster strikes, two normally sane people – who if you asked them individually about their ability to communicate would see no problems on their side – invariably find that they have not understood one another's viewpoints.

But communication has to be continuous, to encompass everyone and to take into account all the implications; otherwise by its very nature it has failed. Yet it is often found that communication channels are invariably built in a haphazard way and tend to fall off, the higher up in the organisation you go. Chief executives and senior management are notoriously bad in the way they communicate their thoughts and ideas to the rest of the organisation. If something is obvious to them, then why cannot the workforce see it too? Similarly, just because an organisation 'knows' its products and services are superior to those of its competitors, why can't every idiot on the high street see that too?

The answer is simple. Each of us is bombarded by information every minute of our lives; so much so that we all take it for granted. Yet we base our decisions to do anything on our experiences, knowledge and feelings – often brought on by a feel-good factor – which, as we've just said, is continually changing. Busy directors may not even realise that their knowledge base could be totally different from that of one of their subordinates and they therefore may overlook to pass on what they regard as total common sense, whereas others might not have the knowledge with which to have come to that conclusion in the first place. And if the company staff are being kept in the dark, what possible hope is there for the customers or suppliers to read the minds of the company directors?

Other reasons for non-communication are many. For instance, many managers still believe that only 'good news' should be told in order to keep up staff morale and to keep customers happy. The problem with this is that bad news invariably leaks out and the rumour-mill is set in motion.

Directors also have a tough time. On the one hand it is illegal to mislead the financial markets with false information, but on the other hand they must guard against private information being used for insider trading.

What on earth is a director or manager to do? For many, it is much easier just to keep quiet and to live in one's own personal cocoon, which results in a workforce that appears remote from the organisation and a management that fails to make the most of the available talent. The potential customers, meanwhile, feel let down by an organisation that appears to care little for them and, in the new world of fast-moving technologies there is absolutely no reason why any customer needs to feel loyalty to any organisation, just because they were a 'captured' client in the past.

So setting up effective communication within any organisation should be structured and implemented from the very highest levels. We all know the classic tale of Rolls-Royce, which failed to listen to its workforce, its suppliers and its competitors, failed to heed the market signs and failed to invest in new engine technology with the result that bankruptcy loomed large and shareholders lost their shirts.

Times have changed a great deal since those days. Faster change is now the norm in most organisations and companies need both to embrace change and to communicate the effects of that change if they are to survive in the modern world and grow their businesses and customer base.

Simply put, non-communication is not an option and poor communication could well lead to corporate death.

ONE

What's It All About?—
Communications and
Language

Business is all about communication – well, to be more accurate, business is all about communication and making money, since there would be little point in a business communicating anything if it didn't make any money.

But in an era dominated by technology and communication channels, what once appeared to be a simple process for all businesses has become ever more complex, such that many companies fail miserably in their communication efforts.

Communications is one of those grand sounding words, which can mean everything and nothing at one and the same time. All businesses need to communicate with their employees if they want the best out of them, with suppliers if they want the right raw materials at the best price, with shareholders if they want to keep them on their side, with customers if they want to make any profit at all, and with the community at large since no one – let alone any company – is an island and can act totally unaffected by the community at large.

Successful communication applies equally to manufacturing industries as it does to service sector or public-sector organisations. Everyone is involved in one way or another but the problem is that few people are taught to communicate in a manner that is suitable for business. In social communication we can afford to be sloppy in what we say since in general both parties know one another and can take it that things left unsaid can be taken as read. (When we use the word 'say' we can equally well mean write, of course, or any of the other forms of communicating that we shall be examining in this book.)

But in a business environment, communication has to be clear, precise and unambiguous and, if you want to avoid being bitten in the bum at some later date, it needs to be formal in nature and planned carefully.

Communication – whether it involves organisations, individuals or groups of individuals – requires a minimum of two parties. Although one party may be the initial sender of a message and the other the initial receiver, both sides need to take on both roles if successful communication is to occur. This is because feedback – even if only a nod of the head – is essential if the sender is to get confirmation that a transaction has been completed.

While writing this book, we were driving along a seven-mile stretch of road in Cambridgeshire one evening and outside every single house were bags of rubbish, which had been left out all day waiting for collection from the dustbin men. It was a week after Easter and quite obviously the collection rotas had been changed for that week to take account of the public holidays. We rang up Huntingdon District Council in whose patch this eyesore had occurred to ask them why no one had apparently been told of the changed collection times. 'We communicated the new collection times to everyone,' we were told by an officious spokesman in the waste operations department. 'They were printed quite clearly in the local paper.' We pointed out that from the look of things, the majority of people obviously didn't get the local paper. 'That's not our fault,' came the reply. 'We communicated the dates and times, but if they don't read the local press, that's not our fault.'

Need we say more? Actually, the following bank holiday a letter from the council was sent to every household giving the times of the collections – addressed to 'the Occupier'. So they took it on board.

The ideas communicated can be either verbal or graphical – verbal in the sense of spoken, written or emailed, for instance, and graphical encompassing any message that can be encapsulated as a visual image. After all, we know that a picture can paint a thousand words (and equally that the best television pictures are on radio, where the mind can conjure up detail hugely superior to a mere TV screen.)

Although these direct channels are essential elements of communication, there are a number of other indirect channels that many businesses ignore, but that can be a major source of poor communication if handled improperly. Think of the importance of body language, for instance. We are all very quick to make instant impressions of people by the way they look or the body signals they give off. Someone who is unable to keep eye contact and is always looking away from you is likely to be giving off indirect signals that they are untrustworthy or certainly not someone you can rely upon, even if the real reason is an outward sign of shyness. Indirect communication channels can also include the environment in which the message is being conveyed, or even the relevance of some comment in the context of the whole message.

Communication can also be prevented or minimised by interference that stops a message from getting through. Extraneous noise, be it someone digging up the road outside, or a protester heckling at a meeting, can often divert the receiver's attention from the real message getting through, but interference in the form of preconceptions on the part of the receiver can also play a major role in a lack of comprehension. If your customers don't trust you as a company because of something they may have heard about you, then it may not matter what you say to them because everything you do say will be treated with cynicism or simply not believed.

So barriers can exist in many different forms, but with the commonality of ensuring that core messages are either hindered or stopped altogether from getting through. Although downsizing has recently played a considerable role in making flatter, more responsive organisational structures, the top-down hierarchy – so beloved in former manufacturing industries especially – was divisive in splitting people both horizontally between departments and vertically between the various layers of management. This gave rise to the 'them and us' attitude so prevalent in the heavily unionised industries of the last century.

A further element of this departmental segregation has been that although people may communicate well within their own department, they may not see the overall picture of what the company is trying to do because they are blinded by the need to fulfil their department's objectives at the expense of other departments that they may see as competitors.

The vertical separators that are epitomised by executive directors devolving power and control to senior managers have only exacerbated the separation between senior directors and the rest of the workforce, resulting in an isolated executive and disgruntled employees, so typified by the nationalised industries that were starting to die out in the 1990s. Yet it's a truism that in many businesses today a large proportion of the people who make up a company have little or no contact with the company's customers and are therefore blind to the problems experienced by the very people who pay their wages – those selfsame customers. Instead, they are too busy fighting for their own position and perks instead of aiming to improve the business generally by serving the customers.

Again, this was typified by the so-called 'fat cat' bosses of the nationalised industries who were on a totally different wavelength from their subordinates, who in their turn distrusted the executives and lapped up the stories of fat-cattery in action as written up in the tabloids. (We remember all too well the CEO of one utility, which is best kept incognito, who quite literally did not know either the name or the position of the person who occupied the office adjacent to his because he used one corridor to access his office while his underling entered the same floor from another doorway. In confidence he admitted that he would feel too embarrassed so late in the day to actually walk around the corridor to find out who was there. 'What if I didn't recognise them?' was his lament!)

The results are clear for anyone who may wish to look. Executives of some companies are well known for communicating their decisions down the corporate ladder with little comprehension of what the impact of those decisions will be, either on the company or on the people who have to implement those decisions. This may well be backed up by executives who fail to adhere to the values they set others and who fail to set measurable performance yardsticks by which others can measure success. In other words, they are bad leaders.

The corollary of this is that managers lack enthusiasm for change; since they have no means of measuring their effectiveness, they may feel stressed in even implementing the executives' wishes. The result is that the rest of the workforce feel unappreciated, have no clear focus and, in that well-worn phrase, feel like mushrooms – left in the dark and having manure thrown at them from on high.

Positive communications cannot survive in a world of hidden and suppressed personal feelings since we all have feelings and everything we do or say is controlled by those feelings. It is surely much better to harness and understand people's feelings and use them in a positive way to help the communication process. After all, even anger is an expression of frustration, and emotional needs have a habit of expressing themselves in one way or another. For open communications to work we need to communicate both positive and negative feelings, since bottling it all up is bound to lead to an explosion at a later time. So it is important to understand that immediate reactions to problems often disguise deeper feelings, which need to be unlocked.

Mind Your Language

Even before the tower of Babel, language has been at the heart of communication. We have all learned to talk from birth and we all think we are terribly good at it. What could be more natural or easier than something we've all done since day one?

Unfortunately, the reality is different. Most of us don't have to cogitate very long to think of people we know who are anything but good communicators.

There are several reasons or categories they fall into – noting that the first three are personal and may not be always correctable, but do cause misunderstandings:

- Speech impediment – whatever its cause this is bound to create a difficulty in comprehension by others.
- Not using their mother tongue, which leads to use of inappropriate tenses, declensions and conjugations.

- Strong regional accents or differences in the use of language on a regional basis.

The correctable areas, which need to be addressed, are:

- Talking in jargon – which most specialist groups tend to do.
- Talking *at* the person with whom they are trying to communicate – but communication, by definition, is a two-way process.
- Malapropisms or misuse of the language out of ignorance – we recently heard a manager regaling a bemused group of builders about the 'JCBs' holding up load-bearing walls.
- Highfalutin or inappropriate use of long or impressive sounding words in order to gain the upper ground – we all know this is simply a load of floccinaucinihilipilification!

It's awful to have a communication problem, but the greater problem is that most of us don't think we have one! Everyone has their jargon and other people are excluded from full understanding of it – mainly their clients or prospective clients. After all, why else would they go to an expert at all? Because they don't know – or don't know enough. Therein lies the need to follow the route to specialists and to money changing hands. 'Tis life, and it makes the world go round.

Take the legal profession, for instance. A more impenetrable minefield for the unwary is hard to imagine. Lawyers and solicitors appear to understand one another, but to the outsider it can all seem unfathomable and can generate mistrust, at the worst, and crossed wires at the very least. Keith Turner, of Northampton-based Turner Coulston, explains it this way:

> *We understand what we're talking about and we have our own language. The trouble is that the public think that the language we use is English, but the truth is that it's not English. It is a legal language, which is designed to be unambiguous, and we use words, the meaning of which we know; whereas if we use colloquial language you can't be sure how a Court will interpret the words. Consequently, we tend to use this specialised language, which looks like English.*

Now it's awfully hard for the lawyer who uses it as a matter of course to understand that the client doesn't understand what he's actually saying. I frequently send documents to people, thinking that I've written them in absolutely plain English – easy to understand – but people then say, 'I can't understand this. It's too difficult.' I try to use commas and not to use heretofores and so on unless I'm writing a document, which is only being read between solicitors. If it is, then it seems to me I can use technical language if I want.

We try really hard to write it in plain English but it is very hard to do so because otherwise you could spend ages trying to think of another way of saying a sentence (which increases the bill), whereas you can say it quickly and cheaply by using a phrase that you know has a particular meaning.

However, Keith Turner has an answer to the problem of under-standing legalese.

I've found that if you want to understand a legal document, the easiest way to do it is to read it out loud – even if it has a lack of punctuation – because the brain puts the punctuation in; and it's incredible how much easier it is to understand if it's read out loud. I say to clients, 'If you're having a problem, read it out loud first and see if it makes sense.' Most times it does.

But people get fazed. It's rather like a long German word. I have absolutely no idea how to start pronouncing it because it seems to go on for ever. It's the same with a legal sentence. The paragraph is 'this long' and your brain is effectively frightened looking at the detail and you automatically jump and can't make sense of it.

A barrister, whom we shall call Nicholas Slater, put it to us this way:

Here's a very short example of something that is impenetrable, however many times you read it. If you're a company lawyer then it may be OK. Even in context it's bad enough. This is a prohibition against giving financial assistance between one related company and another.

Companies Act 1985 Pt V, Ch VI, s155 (5):

Where the financial assistance is to be given by the company in a case where the acquisition of shares in question is or was an acquisition of shares in its holding company, that holding company and any other company which is both the company's holding company and a subsidiary of that other holding company (except, in any case, a company which is a wholly-owned subsidiary) shall also approve by special resolution in general meeting the giving of the financial assistance.

This makes much more sense if you give it the common sense approach of Keith Turner.

Nicholas Slater continued:

The advice you give to anybody to be an effective communicator is first, be sure to get the terms right or second, communicate within your own terms or else third, don't communicate at all. Don't start borrowing anybody else's jargon because you'll always get it wrong. A little learning is a dangerous thing. Some jargon is there to keep outsiders out. Some of it is there because it actually saves a lot of time. It's shorthand for everyone who is 'in'. For instance when a lawyer says, 'We have given our clients certain advice' it actually means 'We're on a hiding to nothing and we know it.'

Do you know the difference between misfeasance, malfeasance and nonfeasance? Misfeasance is doing the wrong thing, malfeasance is doing the right thing but badly and nonfeasance is not doing it at all.

People who use language wrongly usually do so because they think they've got it right. People who talk about 'criteria' and 'phenomena' in the singular think they're being smart and educated and so do people who think 'appraise' means 'apprise'.

Mind you, there are often common-or-garden misquotes . . .

I remember in the Court of Appeal when my witness had said, 'I felt as if the sword of Damocles was hanging over my head.'

This came up in the transcript as 'as if a sort of pantyhose was hanging over my head'! Even the judge found this hilarious. Ignorance sets the balance as you attempt to correct things.

Litigants-in-person appear to be a special breed. Nicholas Slater told us a wonderful story about a 'Mr Gresham' who had been rabbiting away in the Court of Appeal for about an hour when the presiding judge stopped him and said, 'We've been listening with great interest to your submissions but what interests us is the reference that you keep making to the allegations. It would help us if you would be so kind as to identify where those allegations are to be found and who it is who is making them.' And he said, 'My lords, the allegations to which I was alluding to are those at page 64 of the written sub-missions, and I am the alligator'!

As the French expression goes: '*C'est plus facile à parler, qu'à dire quelque chose*', which loosely translated means, 'It's easier to talk than to say something.'

'With respect' is one of those lovely little phrases that means exactly the opposite; just like 'it gives me no pleasure to' – which means 'I'm absolutely thrilled to bits'! Or 'I hear what you say', which means, 'If you say so, but we both know that it's absolute nonsense.'

He continued:

Lawyers will often say 'I am instructed . . .' which means, 'I know this is nonsense, but that's what I've been told to do.' It's like criminals saying 'to be perfectly honest'. I used, in my criminal days, to say. 'Don't say that whatever you do'. Or 'To tell you the truth, gov!' No! No! No! And it's the same between the lawyers themselves. 'As your lordship pleases' means 'I hate you and if you weren't sitting there I'd sort you out!' But of course, judges never make mistakes, as you'd learn if you went to the Court of Appeal. Instead they 'fall into error'.

In a recent case where three different versions of an affidavit had been signed by a defendant, after a lengthy trial containing many conflicting claims by that same defendant, the judge stated in his summary that he had been 'a totally unreliable witness' – which is a very gentle and coded way of saying that he was an out-and-out liar.

But every discipline has its jargon. For instance within banks, following a credit reference request, the receiving bank will respond with coded language for which they cannot be sued, but which makes very clear the financial viability of their client. 'Respectable and trust-worthy and good for your figures and purpose' means simply that you're OK and they've never had any problem with you. 'Respectable and trustworthy' means a slightly less endorsed financial statement whereas 'We are sure that our clients would not commit themselves beyond that which they could see their way clear to fulfil' tells all. The bank is not at all happy about this one.

Likewise the messages put on returned cheques, 'Refer to drawer, please represent' means that he hasn't got the funds at the moment but he probably will have when you present the cheque again. 'Refer to drawer' shuts the door because this client has played the numbers game too often and has simply run out of plausibility rope as far as the bank is concerned.

But back to plain English, because therein lies our comfort zone. Unfortunately we all think that what we say makes sense, but language is full of ambiguity.

Take the word 'by' as used in 'by 1 April'. Does that mean before 1 April starts or on and including 1 April? And what if you live in Yorkshire, where the word 'while' has come to be used to replace 'until'? For instance, a Tyke may well tell you, 'I'll be here while seven o'clock.' And it doesn't take too much brainpower for you to realise that he will be there until seven o'clock. So what happens, you may well ask, when a Yorkshire mum teaches her children not to cross the road at the pelican crossing 'while the green man is flashing'?

Likewise in Wales, there is a different usage of the word 'tidy' from that in the rest of the English-speaking world. People buy and wear clothes 'for tidy' – or as some might say 'for Sunday best'.

In America if something is 'slated' then it is put on the table as being something good to be considered – pretty well the opposite of the meaning found on this side of the Pond.

Linguistic misunderstandings can so easily occur if we remember what Humpty Dumpty said in *Alice in Wonderland*: 'When I use a word, it means just what I choose it to mean – neither more nor less.'

By this alone the response of 'OK' to a statement made in an e-mail could, for instance, mean 'OK, I'll think about it.' Or 'OK, I agree with you.' Depending on what you take the response to mean, your subsequent actions will be totally different, which could lead to totally different outcomes.

Language is at the core of all communications. Roger White, Director of Corporate Affairs at PricewaterhouseCoopers, sums it up like this:

> With any use of language keep it simple. Don't over-complicate. Don't get buried in jargon. That's why everybody thinks that doing communications or PR is easy. Everybody thinks that they can do it. But they can't necessarily. When it's done well it looks easy, but it isn't. Usually if you have done it well it's because you have done it simply.

So let's return to the lawyers for them to have the last word – for they often do:

> There was a young barrister making an impassioned plea in a dog destruction case. The magistrates were going to sentence the dog to death and this young man was saying, 'This isn't the sort of dog that deserves to be put down. Just look at this photograph, and say to yourself, "Is Stan the kind of dog that needs to be taken away from its owner?" Of course he's not. What could be sweeter, what could be nicer, more English, more docile than the very name Stan? Does it not convey to your worships a dog in the bosom of his family running happily around the garden, curling up in his master's lap in the evening in front of the fire, with his loyal loving look and his tender brown eyes? Could you bring yourselves to condemn a dog called Stan?'
>
> And the dock officer said, 'I think I should just point out to your worships and counsel that you may be under a misappre-hension. I think there's been a typing error in his instructions. The dog is in fact called Satan.'

T W O

The Board

The board is the hub and strategic driver of a company and, so that we can see what communications should come from whom, it's important to understand the different roles within the management of a company. The board effectively drives the strategy and the company, whereas the management runs the day-to-day business. The company secretary is servant to the board.

It's the company secretary's job to liaise with solicitors on behalf of the board. They will often be a solicitor themself. The accounts have to be run, and the responsibility to have them submitted, to make sure the directors are doing their job and performing their legal duties and not doing those things that they're not allowed to do, under the Companies Act, lies with the company secretary. In addition, making sure that the shareholders are kept properly informed and that the completion of the annual return and the AGM all go smoothly, are further responsibilities. For example, it is the company secretary who will write the chairman's report on the front of a balance sheet, which puts the best possible gloss on it while the other directors are being told the bad news.

However, as many who attend conferences know, many main board directors are pretty poor communicators themselves. Of the communications needed within the board and between the company and the City, too many people think that many items are confidential when they really don't warrant it; therefore not enough information is given to the City for it to make a judgement. This can be a fine dividing line and can lead to misconceptions.

In order to see how boards can have problems in communication, let's look at the main roles within the board itself.

Most directors have their specific disciplines, and herein lies a potential problem for communication and working well together as a board. Not only do they have their own agendas but they also have their own comfort zones and prejudices. These can make for lively debate – but also misunderstanding.

Finance directors must, of necessity, communicate the financial state of the business both internally and externally. So as well as trying to ensure that their communications are clear, and actually mean what they as individuals are saying (with all their specific jargon and perceptions), it is essential for them to understand the motivation of each of the other directors together with their comfort zones, prejudices and fears.

There seems often to be an affiliation between finance and IT. If the company does not have an IT director then the head of IT is likely to report directly to the FD. This in itself can create a further barrier between the FD and other directors, who see the FD as being the arbiter and controller of ever-changing figures, who has also now donned the mantle of the IT geek. Both of these disciplines can be difficult for other people to understand, which leads to a discomfort that one person is perceived to have more power because of their technological and financial knowledge than the others and may well employ more jargon which makes the others feel excluded.

Sales and marketing directors are often seen as the advocates of spending, without too much tangible evidence of return or projected return. Their perceived agenda is clear: spending without prudence. There is therefore a potential in-built clash between them and the FD.

The role of the managing director or CEO is nearly always that of the manager/leader who drives the motley crew forward in a strategic plan to wow the competition, customers, investors and suppliers alike, all at once. And it can be a very lonely job being a managing director.

To overcome these potential flash points and barriers to success, every board member should focus on:

- The objectives for the company as well as their own discipline;
- Trying not to use jargon; and
- Seeing the other directors' points of view and how they arise.

However, there is another role, which should carry an entirely object-ive view – that of the non-executive director.

To gain an independent view of what makes boards work well, or fail, we consulted Peter Waine, whose experience of working with boards for many years is second to none. He is the CEO of Hanson Green, which specialises in helping boards to function well and which places nonexecutive directors and compiles and directs advisory boards. His knowledge of how boards communicate, and how they do and don't work, is excellent. (His views, in depth, can be found in his book, *The Board Game*, published by Wiley.) He told us that a non-executive director gives a specific balance to the board.

> *Non-executive directors can ask very intelligent questions of their board and ensure that they relate to the concerns of the board, both now and in the future. They can offer tremendous amounts to a board especially if they have an executive post or a post on another board, so that they have something new in their lives. The ability to relate and communicate is what a good non-executive director is all about.*
>
> *Communication forms a most important part of the selec-tion process for a non-exec post ensuring that the third party, who is the potential non-exec, goes through meetings with the chairman and chief executive or the chairman of the nomina-tions committee – because in the end the non-exec has to get on with the chairman and chief executive and – through those two – with the rest of the board.*
>
> *The senior part of any board is the non-executive team – especially when things are difficult and the chairman runs the board and the chief executive runs the company. The non-exec helps to communicate that message on a constant basis, and everyone has to understand that. The non-exec has no career in the company, other than becoming Chairman and therefore they are the only one outside that rarefied world who can talk dispassionately, having chosen the company in the first place.*
>
> *As far as communicating within the company is concerned, the non-exec shouldn't try and second guess, shouldn't try*

and become an executive director in any way whatsoever, shouldn't know as much as the executive directors and so should know how to ask questions at the board. It's not a question of saying, 'You should do this' – it's almost a matter of saying, 'Have you thought about it this way?' and then letting the chief exec take credit for the idea. There shouldn't be any worry from the non-executive thinking, 'I said that and I should get the credit for it.'

The non-exec should be very brave, and very gracious in their communication and say, 'No, this is not right' and be able to say 'No' in a positive way. For instance, at a board meeting, you present a particular policy and I, as non-exec, know that you want that policy carried at that board meeting. But I then say that you know more than I do on the subject of the policy and I know you want it through at this board meeting, but I'm going to say, 'No' and I'm going to convince you that my 'No' is a positive contribution. It may just create a pause rather than a 'No, no, no'. If the rest of the board then comment that the approach that I've taken, as non-exec, has enabled them to think the whole thing through from a different angle, then the non-exec's contribution has been very helpful indeed. You know then that relationship is good and the communication is good.

The attitude is that of wanting to make things happen rather than being the policeman of corporate governance. It is a wonderful post because the non-exec is the confidant, the mentor and the only one, apart from any other non-execs, who has that role. Communication is hugely important in this role.

It can be seen then that a non-exec is actually an enabler within the board and can ensure that the business of the company is conducted in a non-partisan manner while ensuring that communications are really clear. The board without a non-exec director, on the other hand, can be too close to the day-to-day running of the business and may not take the necessary steps back to appraise and then develop the strategies needed for the further development of the company, its market positioning and consequent market share and perception.

Sometimes chairmen are appointed apparently without best practice succession planning. We set the following scenario for Peter Waine: A non-executive chairman is parachuted in to an AIM-listed company because of his previous experience in an executive role and in taking a business to a float. There then proves to be a most dreadful clash of personalities and argument about roles between him and the chief executive, leading to an impasse and clash on the board, which results in the resignation of the chairman. How should you communicate this to the City, shareholders and other audiences? Peter Waine:

A non-exec should not be flown in to rectify a technical imbalance on the board. For a chairman to be flown in because the company has never been through a float, takeover or mergers means that the succession planning hasn't quite worked out and so communication, along with building relationships, is going to be vital to the success.

If a chairman has really been flown in, done a good job but with a heavy price, vis-à-vis the relationship with the chief executive then, in the end, the chairman is the more important of the two. The chairman is the top person. You might say that is a bold thing to say when you see some of the chairmen there are around. The chairmanship is a sinecure for a lot of the time but when the chips are down, he is the most important person. Nobody else can undertake that role. Often when the chips are down, a good chairman will outperform his own expectations. The chairman should not be sacrificed just because the chief executive doesn't like what is happening and the chairman is behaving like a chairman.

If the chairman has to resign because the board isn't going to do the right thing, then he is in a very powerful position. A chairman doesn't get pushed out unless he's done something wrong and the non-execs don't think he has done the right thing. If he has done the right thing but the chief exec doesn't want him any longer, then you have very weak non-execs. The best and ultimate sanction of a non-exec, which communicates very clear messages both inside and outside the company, is to resign. If you are resigning and subsequently vindicated then you will be noticed in the City and respected for it.

In communication terms the mere fact that he's resigned has communicated a lot – he hardly need do any more. He then needs to go on holiday for a couple of weeks and not be contactable so that things settle. That's fundamental. Then you must consider that he's probably communicated quite a lot prior to the resignation – these things are not generally unexpected and totally out of the blue. He'd be unwise to say much more than the fact that he's left that board.

He still owes a duty of loyalty to the company and, presumably an interim chairman will be appointed. It is that interim chairman who should be interviewed by the press to see what's different. It isn't the resigning chairman's role to communicate on that any more after the resignation.

In essence, the ones who have resigned have actually changed the companies simply by not being there anymore – and often for the good. The power of the communication of their resignation will have tightened up the rest of the board anyway. I can't think of an example when a non-exec has resigned without it having done the company good because of it.

If all this sounds overly involved, Peter Waine is keen to point out that on the whole we communicate well in this country. The evidence can be seen in the results – after all, the UK is the fourth biggest economy in the world, with 1% of its population owning 8% of the world's wealth, and we export more per head than any other country in the world. There's an awful lot of talent in the UK.

However, even with the best of intentions, communications often fail even at board level simply because people don't talk to one another at the appropriate times. This failure is a mixture of lack of strategy as well as communication. Take this tale from a woebegone IT director who learned his lesson well! He prefers to remain anonymous . . .

Last year we decided to install an intranet. Now, my depart-ment all know about intranets – IT people talk intranets and we all instantly know what they're about. We know what they can do and what benefits they can offer. We may not be able to estimate the exact cost savings, but we know there is benefit to be gained.

I sold the idea to our finance director. I did the proposal, said what it was going to do and how much it would cost, and he bought into it. We were then due to see the chief executive who effectively holds sway over the final decision, but he couldn't make the meeting and therefore never found out what we were going to do. So we kicked off the project anyway (because my FD can sign things off) and so we were off and running.

At the next operational board meeting we had by now kicked off the intranet project and suddenly, in front of them all, the CEO piped up, 'Why do we need this?' So suddenly I was on the back foot. How could he say that? We had sent the papers to him, had asked him to attend a meeting, so we could tell him all about it, but he had missed it; and in the middle of that board meeting he then came up with a question like that.

Because it threw me so much, I remember thinking, How do I explain what an intranet is and what the benefits could be? But you don't get that amount of time in a board meeting. It would have taken too long. The problem occurred then because the operations division hold a lot of sway over what happens. They said, 'So here we are spending a lot of money and no one knows why we're doing it.' I was protesting that we were going to benefit, and talked about what it would offer, but as an intranet is not the easiest of concepts to grasp they were not sure about this.

The communication had obviously broken down right there. What should have happened was that when the CEO did not turn up to the meeting, we should have gone to see him to get him up to speed and get him to buy into it. Instead, what happened was that other people took his lead in that meeting.

There are eight area directors who all hold an opinion and all need to be convinced of the argument. We had talked to a few of them before the meeting and one of them had agreed to be the sponsor of the project, which was great because if we hadn't got him on side initially it could well have been that he would have been kicking dirt in our faces along with the others. So in the end I was pleased that he did actually turn into our champion and the project continued – but it was a close call.

I find this is quite a common scenario in small businesses where people are playing politics. If the CEO had said first of all in the meeting that he was behind the project, the others would most likely have got behind him and supported the whole thing. What happened in this case was that he was the ultimate authority and everyone else thought, 'Let's get behind him and give IT some hassle!' Where the lines of demarcation aren't established in smaller businesses that are growing as fast as ours and where responsibilities can move and change daily, then you find that there's no obvious line where people can say, 'Well, that's IT's responsibility.'

So to reiterate, you can see that there was an alliance between the IT director and the main board FD and because of this the two of them assumed that there would be enthusiasm on the part of the rest of the board for the proposed scheme. In fact, there was egg on faces because while the perceived priority was to get the project started, the real priority was to get the real decision-maker on board by good communication.

To analyse this situation, and prescribe the best practice:

- Be aware of alliances and allow for them in your planning.
- Ensure that everyone involved in the decision-making is fully informed in good time.
- Don't assume that anything is a given.
- Get someone outside of your discipline to read your proposal, to ensure that jargon doesn't cloak the message.
- Lobby and get feedback prior to raising your head above the parapet.
- Don't be proud. If the feedback dictates that you review the proposal, be prepared to look at it critically and realistically.

The Chairman Who Chose What Not to Communicate

Although everyone is agreed that 'honesty is the best policy', there are times when it pays to be 'economical with the truth', or at the very least to time one's communications precisely in order to gain maximum advantage.

The following story was told to us by the chairman of a well-known plc, which, because of the sensitivity of the information, must remain anonymous. This chairman (whom we'll have to call 'Mr X') found himself in a very difficult situation, which tested his resolve and his moral fibre to the limit. We make no moral judgements here. However, when you have read his story, think what you might have done in the circumstances – what you might have communicated to whom, when you would have decided to become economical with the truth – knowing all along that your brief was to sell the company well, and aware of the responsibilities incumbent on a chairman.

Hostile Bid

The company, which was a good business, was turning over a little less than £4m but it had been making about £500 000 pre-tax profit, bottom line. Mr X told us:

We'd only been involved for a couple of years and there was a hostile bid for the company in the sum of just over £16m, which was very attractive, as such. The board having discussed the bid were persuaded that it was absurd to accept that bid as it stood; but that we should put the company to market in the circumstances. I was asked if I would take that job on as no one else on the board had any experience of that.

Mr X went to check out costs, etc. with one of the major stockbroking firms who could have handled the deal. They indicated that it would total around £500 000. The board agreed that that was far too costly for a small company and that they should do it themselves. Accordingly Mr X was asked to lead the team.

Step 1

The first stage they had to go through was to identify the names of all the potential serious purchasers who had resource and could have logical reasons for being interested in their company. They came up with about 30 names, drawn from within the confines of the UK and Europe, which they felt was the most likely area in which to find the right bidder. Mr X again:

> We prepared a two-page simple synopsis of the highlights of the business – enough to whet appetites – just a series of commercial paragraphs describing the business. I immediately telephoned each of the chief executives and/or chairmen of each of those businesses, explained the situation and said I would send them a confidential letter if they could make sure it could get it into the right hands. I asked them if they would like to receive such a letter – and, of course, most people said, 'Yes'. (In that circumstance they had nothing to lose, and they could learn something about what was going on.) So it was fairly straightforward to get those letters into the right hands.
>
> From that I got 10 or 12 responses, which were positive indications of interest, wanting to go further forward. This formed the nucleus of our plan.

Step 2

The next step that the team had to go through – subject to the appropriate confidentialities – was to provide more detailed information in order to enable those interested to decide whether or not they were interested enough in going to the stage of funding due diligence.

Mr X explained to the interested parties that the process at that stage would be as follows:

1. Anyone who said they wanted to go to due diligence would be given a due diligence room of their own in the company's lawyers' offices and would be allowed a maximum of two days for due diligence.

2. At the end of that due diligence they would either withdraw or they would put in a binding firm offer.

This was a fairly aggressive timetable, but in this case the company's affairs were extremely clean and everything was provided in the data room such that they could draw upon it in that two-day period. We were dealing with very substantial companies, of course, pretty well throughout.

The data that was sent to them, to enable them to take the decision to go to due diligence or not, was such that three of them decided to go ahead. Arrangements were made for them to come in on separate days and have the financial director and the company's lawyers available as necessary for the due diligence periods.

As a result of those due diligences, all three made offers. A key point was that, while those offers were legally binding on them, I made it clear that they would not be legally binding on us and that as far as we were concerned, they would be taken only as an invitation to us to either proceed or not proceed. (Obviously they didn't know how many they were up against.) All I had told them was that we had sent out invitations to 10 to 12 companies, and hopefully they were going to think there were seven or eight in the frame. At the end of the exercise I had three parties, none of whom had any idea how many other parties were involved and who had all made legally binding offers. The exercise then became one of how to handle each of those three situations.

Preferred Bidders and Miscommunication

The next critical milestone in such a situation is when the company decides to go forward with what is called a 'preferred bidder'. They have to tell the other 'hopefuls' that they are not preferred bidders and at that stage the other two will probably walk away from the deal. For Mr X's company, this is where the danger zone started.

The preferred bidder is left on his own and is then in a position where he can play ducks and drakes with you if he wants to and the result is that you are exposed. My whole strategy was to avoid exposure and the risk of losing a deal as much as I humanly could. So I had to keep my cards close to my chest – critically so. I also threw in some jokers from time to time to put people off the scent. So I was actually communicating irrelevant pieces of apparently comforting data. The objective was to encourage a suitor to feel that he was well in with the pack and equally to encourage him to feel that he might miss out because his price wasn't quite as good as it needed to be – but without telling any fibs in the process. That was important because of one's credibility.

A number of conversations took place. Miscommunication had a critical effect on the perception of the non-preferred bidders about the unknown number of parties who were committed. One of those parties had offered slightly in excess of £22m for the business against the £16m that had been offered by the hostile bidder in the first place. The other two had offered sums upwards of £19.5m. On the basis of that, the preferred bidder was going to give the company about £22 million.

Mr X called a board meeting to formalise what he had been doing and to recommend that they should accept that offer, and the board acknowledged this to be the right course of action.

Timing Is All

I duly got on to the preferred bidder, told him that he was the preferred bidder and left it as long as I could before telling the other two that they were not the preferred bidders. (I had indicated on the timetable to all parties the date on which we would have the board meeting to make the decision and the timing with which I would give them an answer.) That left me as much breathing space as possible for me to get on with the preferred bidder in a rush to get past the post. We started work on that particular Tuesday afternoon with the preferred bidder, which involved a lot of legal work on both sides.

Interestingly, at about 8 p.m. on that Tuesday evening I received a phone call from the chairman of a large public company whose group had an equity interest in one of the other failed bidders. He had heard that their minority interest in the unsuccessful bidder had failed. He said to me that, on behalf of the parent, they wanted to make an offer. I pointed out that they had effectively missed the boat because it was past our closing date and the board had agreed to go with another preferred bidder; whereupon he pointed out to me that, not withstanding that, I had an obligation to protect the interest of the shareholders of my company, and I should give my company's shareholders the best deal and the best returns on their investment – which is also quite true.

Moral Dilemma

As the chairman handling these negotiations, it's also incumbent upon me to ensure certain other litmus tests are taken – such as looking after the long-term interests of the employees, assessing whether a bidder is going to close the whole thing down and get people put out of work, for example. Also, is the reason for the acquisition likely to be something nefarious in some way or another, offering no particular future to the business? What are the best interests of the creditors and all the different parties to the business? Their interests are supposed to be considered. However, the one that weighs most heavily of all is seeing what's the deal that gives the best return for the shareholders.

Mr X explained to us that he had to be seen to be giving due consideration to all these other issues as well. At the end of the day he had just to ask the right questions of the parties who were bidding and hope to get honourable answers from them. One had to assume that their intentions were honourable. If they were not and they didn't give the right answers, one could only say that one had done one's best.

I acknowledged to that chairman that if what he said had substance, and he was going to be making an offer that I would have difficulty in refusing, then I had to listen to what he had to say and reflect upon it. He, in fact, came in and said he wanted to offer £25m, which of course was £3m more than we had previously been offered. It was fairly obvious to me that he, shall we say, had some inside information in order to determine where to put his bid in – correctly, of course. The directors who had been present at our board meeting in the morning actually included the chairman of the company that had made the hostile bid in the first place, and shared the equity interest with this bidder. He would easily have been in a position to pass on that information, though it would, of course, have been improper for him to have done so. But people do talk.

Because the figure of £25m was so much in excess of the earlier figure being offered quite correctly, I had no alternative but to give it very serious consideration. That put me in a very difficult position. I was pursuing, in good faith, negotiations with one public company and we were both employing lawyers to do work; both on the basis of being 'at risk' – the same principle of selling a house in England until it is completed – but at the same time having to consider this new bid of £25m.

The problem that Mr X now felt was that, thinking it through, it's perfectly possible that the new offer could have been what's known as a 'spoiling bid'. In other words, offer £25m, get the other party to go away so you get a clear field and then suddenly say, 'We've changed our minds; we don't like it after all.' So on reflection, he rang back the chairman of the public company and made the point about the possibility of a spoiling bid that he couldn't take a risk on, but at the same time acknowledged that this figure would put him as the preferred bidder, assuming it had real substance.

Put Your Money Where Your Mouth Is

I indicated to him that the only thing that had occurred to me that I could use as a validating factor was if he was to lodge a nonreturnable deposit of £9m in my company's bank account – which he duly agreed to do because it was probably a safe way of showing genuine intent from both points of view. I said that as soon as my bank confirmed that the amount was in the account I would tell the other party that the after-time bid had taken preference. Meanwhile I had to keep very silent to the other party, who worked all through the night with their lawyers as did ours to be seen to complete the obligations. I had no option but to be effectively double-faced and to continue to protect my shareholders' interests.

The board could have overridden my decision to have stayed with the other bid, although they would have been on very tricky grounds for doing so. If they had overridden my earlier decision at the board meeting to sell the company because they had taken the view that they could have done better for the shareholders by driving the company forward, then they would have had stronger grounds, because they would have had to justify why they should turn down £20-odd million in order to drive on. In theory, I should have gone back to the board to get the board's approval to change horses. In practice, for a variety of commercial reasons, that really wasn't a practical option. First there were potentially hostile directors on the Board, second the matters were exceptionally sensitive and third, had any of the directors been aware of what was going on, it would possibly have disrupted the opportunity of getting a lot of extra money for the shareholders – which I regarded as my primary responsibility.

Mr X told us that by this time he felt himself to be sailing in slightly uncharted waters. He had a discussion with the company's lawyer and they then waited overnight to have the substance of the new party's £25m bid. Unfortunately, complications arose the following morning.

Horse Trading

At about 11 a.m., the chairman rang back to say that the Stock Exchange yellow book has a clause in it that says that the board were only entitled to vest money into our account, on a non-returnable basis, up to a sum that had some geared relationship to the level of profits that they had last audited. Because of that, the maximum that they could lodge without a reference to the shareholders was about £3m. I commented, 'Well, that does make a big difference.' My private calculations were that I was prepared to accept enough money such that if the deal fell foul and I lost all bidders, the amount that I had gained would have meant that, even going into another round and bidding again, I would still have come out on the right side of the line against the £22m.

So as long as I could sell the business for £13m, with his £9m in the pot if all had failed (and the business was clearly worth more than that), I needed to be sure of getting more than I had already been offered irrevocably. However, he was offering only £3m, which was all he could actually legally offer without all the extra time constraints that would have been involved in getting this verified. The whole exercise had to be done in an enormous rush because otherwise the deal would have gone away. So I told him that his £3m was not good enough because I needed to be sure that he couldn't back off from the deal. I suggested that we should both go and think, and come back again. Meanwhile, the deal continued moving forward with the other party.

I came back to him a little later on that morning with a bright idea, which had been hatched between the lawyer on our side and myself. They were going to have to make an announcement to the Stock Exchange in the usually carefully phrased terms. I therefore proposed that they should put that announcement together and send it to me, and that they should put the £3m nonreturnable deposit into our company's account, that I should be empowered to release that statement to the Stock Exchange Council and they would have no right of redress.

The statement basically told the Stock Exchange Council that they had completed the purchase of the company on the stated terms and conditions. This meant that they couldn't back off from the deal without it severely embarrassing their company to have released such a statement to the Stock Exchange and then to tell the Stock Exchange they hadn't meant what they had said.

After a hurried board meeting they agreed to that scheme because they couldn't think of a better idea. All that took place during Wednesday. Late that afternoon the company's bank confirmed that £3m had been received into its bank account and they were given an irrevocable letter from the new bidder addressed to the Stock Exchange and empowered only for Mr X to release. At this point they became the preferred bidder.

Regrets? I Had a Few . . .

Mr X explained to us that the worst moment of the deal from his point of view was when he had to ring the chairman of the other company, with whom he had got on very well, to say that regrettably there had been a change and they were no longer the preferred bidder. He was apparently very upset.

But then again, Too Few to Mention . . .

I don't think he thought too highly of me and on moral grounds I didn't either. But it was one of those things that you have to do because that's what you're being paid to do. It was the correct and proper procedure to adopt. (I haven't seen him since then, so I don't know how he will see me when next we do meet, but I hope we can be friends.) Anyhow, he said to me that he would have to reflect on his position and have a board meeting and decide what to do, and he would come back to me. Well, he came back to me at about 6 p.m. on the Wednesday evening to say that the board, having considered their position, were prepared to increase their offer to something like £23.5m and that was as far as they were prepared to go. They added that they would withdraw their offer at midday on Thursday if it hadn't been accepted. I said I acknowledged that and 'I hear you and thank you.'

Smoke and Mirrors

Meantime I had spoken to the chairman of the other new public company – the group bidding £25m – and told them that they had now become the preferred bidder and that they should put their legal team to work immediately so that this matter could be resolved very rapidly. (The board of our company were, of course, still under the impression that we were selling the business for £22m.) I then had the new group beavering away and I then told them – after I had got their money and had sent off their statement letter to the Stock Exchange – that they were now the preferred bidder. They were very pleased about that.

I then said to the chairman of the new group that in order not to develop this into an absurd Dutch auction, I proposed that we should have a deadline to the bidding process – that would be 5 p.m. tomorrow, Thursday. I stated that all interested parties could put in their final offer by a dedicated fax with lawyers present at either end to see fair play up until the designated time. This put the new group in a difficult position. The chairman was absolutely furious with me. He said, 'We've bid you an offer that is way ahead of anybody else and there-fore we've won the bidding.' But I told him that he had made an offer that had put him as the preferred bidder and 'You can't expect me just to slam the door on everybody else any more than the door had originally been entirely slammed on you. At 5 p.m. tomorrow you can make your final offer as can every-one else.'

They weren't pleased, but they saw the logic of it; but what worried them was that in the same way that they had, how-soever, found out what the offer they were against was – in order to put in the £25m – they clearly felt that I might equally tip off the other lot and say, 'Hey fellas, just up your bid beyond £25m and come back into the frame again.' Understandably, they were scared stiff that I was going to tip off the other lot. What they didn't know was that the other lot had already been defeated! Obviously I wasn't going to tell them.

Game, Set and Match

So there we were at 5 p.m. on Thursday evening, with everyone feeling thoroughly dead since there had been no sleep since Tuesday morning. The other lot had already packed up and gone home and the bidding group were fighting against themselves. As a result of this, they had to decide what to do about their £25m bid. It was a fascinating thing to stand by the dedicated fax machine at 5 p.m. on Thursday evening with one group of lawyers chatting to their counterparts, wherever their lawyers were, and saying, 'Yes, we're ready to receive now; fair play this end, fair play your end'; and out came the fax, which said £28m!

We duly rang them up. And then I received a phone call from the chairman of that group congratulating me on selling an excellent company and I congratulated him on being a successful bidder. And £28m of clean cash changed hands. That was the deal.

If lessons are to be learned from this whole episode, they are:

- Keep a cool head.
- Think like a chess player through to the endgame.
- Don't rush into saying something you might regret later.
- Get good professionals around you.
- Keep the team small.
- Think what you have to communicate rather than what you could.
- Tell the truth – not necessarily all of it.

THREE

Internal Communications

The middle of the nineteenth century saw a turning point in the evolution of mankind with the dawning of the Industrial Revolution. With the rise of steam power and all the spin-offs that followed in its wake, a crucial point had been reached – a point of no return, which brought riches to some and changed the lives of millions for ever.

The impact of this became part of normal, everyday life with clusters of people living around their places of work in much the same way as they had gathered around the rural economic centres in days of yore. Throughout the twentieth century, what had been local and regional market towns and centres became more national and international as business grew more global and the concept of communications as a force within business became a reality.

With the passing of the twentieth century, a new revolution – no less significant, fired by the breakneck development of computing power – has already stretched its fingers into every walk of life. Its social and economic consequences are already huge, but no one knows for sure where or when it will lead, for it will more than likely open the door for the next revolution – whatever that may be.

In short, any human skills, processes or procedures that can be compressed into a computer's algorithm could eventually be replaced by electronics. Much has been written about the hardships and challenges thrown up by the resulting shift in employment patterns; of the downsizing and deskilling of processes that have for so long relied on the incalculable ingenuity of the human brain; but the arrival of this electronic age has also produced far-reaching implications for the way companies work and in particular how one company differentiates itself from another.

The struggle for competitive edge, however, far from sidelining the workforce, now demands that staff are much more important than ever they had been; for without their empathy, their individuality, their flexibility, creativity and intuitive thinking, there is little to differentiate one business from another. The well-worn phrase that seems to trip unerringly from every chief executive's lips into the depths of the company's annual report – 'Our staff are our most important asset' – has actually taken on a new meaning.

With the death of the job-for-life concept, the need for good, effective internal communications has never been greater. Delivering the goods depends on a director's ability to harness the ideas and creativity of his staff; yet those that remain after a company has been forced to downsize its employees are only too aware of their own vulnerability and frailty within the jobs market. They need to be fired up, to be encouraged to behave in a way that supports the long-term ambitions of the organisation.

Employees have needs and aspirations that need to be met if the directors and senior management want to get the best out of them. Yet too often there is an obvious rift between the majority of the workforce and the upper echelons of management, and frequently this can end up with the customers being the ultimate losers.

How often have you seen examples of management attempting to communicate at, rather than with, their people? Such a situation is rife across all sectors of business, and is even practised by so-called 'enlightened' managers, who can't see that the agenda they set is simply a one-way process of communication.

For too many years, companies have ignored internal communications while hundreds of thousands of pounds have been spent on advertising and image-raising among external audiences. Only now are directors beginning to understand that the traditional safe, comfortable and control-obsessed cultures of the past are, in part, becoming a millstone round the corporate neck: those cultures that saw staff in terms of head count or pairs of hands rather than strategic assets. Secretive cultures based on the need-to-know concept created their own spin-off: the no-need-to-bother attitude.

Within large companies over the past 50 or so years, before the radical downsizing of the early 1990s, there was a great deal of mis-information passed up and down the chain of command. Middle managers protected their little empires, shop-floor staff congregated and acted in herds, while the 'elitist' bosses were perceived as having little concept of what life was really like among 'the workers'.

There was an oft-quoted phrase that 'It's lonely at the top'. It certainly could be for the chief executive of a plc or a multinational; but it can apply equally today to the one-man-band working in his telecottage or his home or hot-desking as a consultant. So perhaps it was surprising that profitability was ever as high as it was.

Just take a minute, then, to think how much better it could all have been had there been a company-wide culture, wherein all employees could have felt free to make constructive suggestions for the common good of the firm.

The objective is that every company can draft its own best practice blueprint for communication. Internal communication is such a key part of that, that this section of the book is quite extensive. It is all too easy to think that you have to communicate with the legal department only if you have a legal problem or need a contract, or with house services only if the loo is blocked. But that is wrong.

Making decisions to impart one batch of knowledge to a specific group of people on a 'need-to-know' basis is also likely to be a hiding to nothing. In principle the best practice communications blueprint will mean that the bulk of general information is available to every-body in the organisation, with the exclusions being as few as possible. Internal communications, whatever their origin, are normally distrib-uted through two specific channels: the communication department and human resources. Both departments must work hand in hand for effective internal communications to take place.

Figure 3.1 is aimed at being an aide-mémoire only, but you need to think very carefully before you exclude any of your internal colleagues from general communications. It is not necessarily right for your company. It's meant to be a crib sheet only and you must create your own, tailor-made to fit your circumstances.

Now you can build the basis for the company-wide culture that is so desirable. To move forward into such a state of nirvana, however,

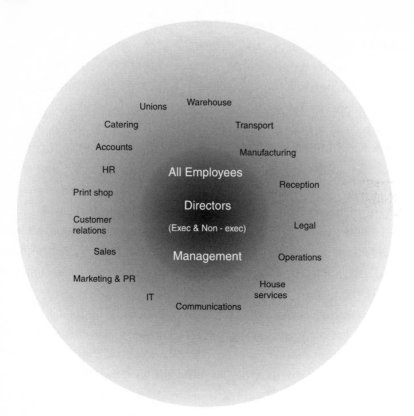

Figure 3.1 *Internal communications*

there needs to be a rationale and purpose established within the company's own set vision and goals, which creates the environment in which lively, creative communications can grow throughout the company. Encouraging, managing, directing and harnessing the creative potential of the workforce are the real challenges of internal communications.

For true bipartisan communication to take place, there needs to be the means for employees to feel that they too can set the agenda, allowing them to bring to the fore problems that they face or anticipate, and allowing – nay, encouraging – them to be discussed openly and honestly. Only that way can customer service ever really be effective, since problems faced by those at the sharp end of the business need to be addressed quickly if customers are not to become aware of internal trouble within the organisation.

'Human Remains'

As one of the main channels responsible for internal communications, it's as well to be able to understand how the human resources function impacts the company as a whole. We turned to international HR consultancy West Associates and spoke to their managing director, Andrew West, for an idea of how the typical HR department views internal communication.

> *My take on internal communications is that honesty is the best policy. It just amazes me how much people will accept and how much bad news you can give them if they are well informed. Perversely some people even seem to thrive on it. I've seen it happen. But it's got to be done honestly. Once you lose credibility, that's it.*
>
> *In my experience, many HR departments communicate too little and they're only too happy to hand over to the communications department. HR people tend to see themselves more as the technicians handling pay schemes and selection whereas the PR people are seen as the spin guys whose job function is to put the message across.*

Maybe this is why HR departments are often regarded simply as penpushers and a questionable overhead – in charge of 'remains' rather than the 'resources'? Andrew West again:

> *Having said that, all the research shows that it is the quality of the manager that makes all the difference, rather than the means of communication. The quality of a manager's relationship with his or her team is key to employee's feelings of well-being, satisfaction and performance. So one of the main roles of an HR manager is to organise the training of managers in interpersonal skills and communications and then to put in place systems, which allow good management and communications to take place.*
>
> *I feel many people can go through virtually anything as long as they know what is happening and feel they have a place and*

they belong within the company. People in adversity are frightened that something is going to happen, and living with ambiguity is a hard thing to do. So the more information you can give them, within reason, the better they're going to feel about it. But more than that, if you say we're all in this together – I'm a chief executive or HR director or whatever, and I'm as much in the firing line as anybody else – then you can focus as a team on the real issues.

There's a syndrome you see quite commonly within companies. Just as everyone thinks they're a good driver, every HR person believes they're a good communicator. But many are arrogant and don't make good listeners. The trouble with the HR function is that it is desperately trying to establish its credentials and move away from the old avuncular 'pay and rations' image. HR people regularly try to say to everyone else, 'We have something to offer' and they're told, 'Get away with you', so they look for credibility in terms of quick fixes and buzzwords rather than looking in depth at substantial issues. Managing HR looks fairly straightforward on the surface but to really improve an organisation's performance through its people is extremely difficult.

In order to develop an effective strategy encouraging two-way employee communication, senior management needs to create an environment in which this type of interaction will thrive. This invariably means ensuring that there is commitment to full internal communication all the way through the organisation and that all employees are empowered to an appropriate degree in implementing company policy.

An employee survey is one way of gauging where to start in this process and this can be carried out using an intranet with emailed answers to a central processing department, or alternatively using paper-based forms.

Anonymity is the key here, and your people must be convinced that what they say won't be held against them in the future, or else the whole exercise will be a waste of time. For this reason, it is common to use outside survey firms who can guarantee anonymity and impartiality.

A typical basic employee survey appears in the next section. Be prepared, though, if you do open the Pandora's box not only to read the answers, but do something about them as well!

One company with whom we were involved in running an employee survey found that there was such dissatisfaction in the Benelux countries that eventually the US parent sold off that part of the company.

Note that just because a company has gone to the lengths of having a written policy of employee empowerment and of full internal communication, all will be for nothing if those at the top of the hierarchical tree don't live and breathe that policy themselves.

We've all come across those naff mission statements that run along the lines of the much-quoted, 'Our employees are our greatest asset'. But how many organisations actually treat the workforce in a way that makes them believe such statements? At the time of the massive downsizing of British utility companies in the 1990s, such mission statements as the one above were commonplace; yet with the workforces being laid off thousands at a time, what messages did the executive think they were sending out internally both to those who were being made redundant and, perhaps more importantly, to those who were left behind, wondering when their turn would come for the big chop? Or what thought was given to work-life balance, rather than the technology being used as a big stick with which to beat the workforce into greater productivity?

A company must have a clear view of the HR department's role in communication as well as that department being able to deal with private, one-to-one staff issues effectively and sensitively. To devise your own best practice blueprint these matters need to be realised:

- The matters that can be dealt with only by HR;
- Full involvement with the development of the internal communication plan (ICP);
- Areas where there may be a conflict of interest or where the message needs to be defined and discussed prior to firming up the ICP;

- Specific concern and focus on how the company's information cascade system works with any dependencies identified;
- A communication path with the communications department regarding staff movements; and
- Close involvement in the purpose, design and implementation of the company-wide intranet.

A Typical Employee Survey

First to gather some demographic information you could ask your people to complete the following:

Level of management – for example

- Execs, vice-presidents, regional vice-presidents and directors
- Managers
- All other employees
- Function
- HR
- Finance and administration
- Operations
- Marketing
- Sales

Location

Length of Service

Less than two years
Two to five years
Six to ten years
Longer than ten years

Age

Less than 25
25 to 34

35 to 44

45 to 54

Greater than 55

And then for each of the following questions select and indicate one of the seven options:

1. Strongly agree
2. Agree
3. Just agree
4. Not sure
5. Just disagree
6. Disagree
7. Strongly disagree

- This is a good company to work for.
- I understand the company's goals and priorities.
- The company has a good reputation in Europe.
- I am confident in the future of the company.
- Senior management does a good job of managing the company overall.
- My function is well managed.
- I feel loyal to the company.
- My manager makes me feel involved and consulted.
- My manager gives me recognition for good work.
- My manager helps me do a good job.
- My manager treats me with respect.
- I like my job.
- My work is interesting and challenging.
- I have the resources I need to do my job.
- I am trusted to do a good job and make the right decisions.
- The company employees all work together towards a common goal.
- The people I work with make an effective team.
- I work in a happy and friendly environment.
- My skills are fully used.
- I feel motivated to do a good job.

- I have sufficient training to do my job.
- There are good opportunities for promotion.
- Policies and procedures are applied effectively and fairly.
- People issues are handled well.
- My total remuneration (pay plus benefits) is competitive.
- I am satisfied with my basic pay.
- I am satisfied with my company benefits.
- My working hours are reasonable.
- The pressure on me at work is reasonable.
- My working environment is acceptable.

If you want to get some genuine individual feedback and the budget will allow for it, you could ask some killer questions such as:

- What do you really dislike about this company?
- What do you like best about this company?
- If you could choose, what one thing would you change?

Don't forget to give feedback on the analysis of the results – ensuring that confidentiality is maintained, or your next survey will not yield much of any use. Done properly, this type of survey can produce loads of useful information, which can have a very positive affect on staff morale.

Strategising Your Communications

Putting it simply, organisational culture is based just as much on the ways in which the executive and senior management behave as it is on what they say. So when your communications department is planning any type of communications strategy, it needs to be based both on the culture of the business and on a true and frank appraisal of any barriers to communication that exist within the organisation.

A communications strategy needs to encompass many things if it is to be successful, and needs to be developed, implemented and run by the communications department in close liaison with all other areas of business. For a start it needs to reflect a culture in which values are of more importance than mere words mouthed as in a mission statement. But most importantly a consistency of communication across the company is vital if messages are to be trusted and people are to understand and play their full role in any changes that will affect both themselves and the company.

So in putting together such a plan, it needs to be sufficiently detailed to define what media are to be used throughout the organisation, ensuring at the same time that it is the strategy that defines the media, rather than the media dictating what strategy is to be implemented. Often enough this will encompass real, face-to-face communications, which should form the backbone of any communications strategy within the organisation. Of course, it must also take cognisance of anything that might enable conflicting messages to be sent out, as well as establishing some kind of measure of how successful those communications are.

The problem with any organisation is that from day one there is already an informal communications network in place, regardless of what management sets out to do. It's called the gossip network and it's fed by rumour. It is therefore essential that your strategy is able to work with this or counteract it effectively, and the best method of doing this is to ensure that your people are empowered to give feedback and positive suggestions throughout the communication networks and that the feedback is actually acted upon.

This means that questions and comments should be actively encouraged and that – where possible – information should be made freely available so that employee trust is built up over time. This should also help prevent another potential communications minefield – one that we have seen countless times. Managements in companies large and small are quite good at sending out messages to external audiences – such as shareholders or even end-users and customers – that are totally different from the messages given out to internal staff. Sometimes that may be necessary, such as when a company is going through difficult times that it needs its people to understand but which, for obvious reasons, it doesn't want leaked to the outside world.

But in the main, there need to be steps taken to ensure that the internal communications implementation and the messages given out externally by the public relations department are in sympathy with one another. After all, the old expression that your employees are (or should be) your best ambassadors means that you can be pretty sure that internal messages will somehow get out. If they conflict with information given out by your PR department, then the credibility of your organisation is bound to suffer – as well as the morale of your people, who will begin to question what they have been told in the first place. This, if for no other reason, is why internal communications are best driven by the communications department as a whole, rather than delegating it to others such as HR, who of course should have a major input to the plan.

These are points to bear in mind:

- Simple is good.
- The old questions, 'Why?' and 'What do you want to achieve?' should be asked before any communication plan item is formulated.
- Communications overload is easy to get into and is just as damaging to a company as shortage of information.
- Bear in mind everyone else's agenda.
- The communications department should make real friends with (and strong allies of) the HR department.

Don't Shoot the Messenger

Sometimes, though, the communications department gets the blame when in fact it is nothing whatsoever to do with them. Take the case of a reorganisation, for instance. Many people do not like change, and certainly they hate uncertainty, especially when it affects their own conditions. Often they will tend to blame poor communications when the heart of the problem lies somewhere else. If people aren't treated with respect or are expected to do things without proper explanation, then it doesn't matter how well they are 'communicated' with; they will still blame the messenger rather than the message.

In essence, the real benefits of employee communications result from getting the listening right, rather than telling people what's going on from the top of the organisation. After all, it's the front-line staff who are often closest to any customer problems, and if you don't listen to them, they may be frustrated, feel badly treated and won't know the information that the customers really want. By listening to what they want to say, you will have a better-motivated workforce, serve your customers better in the process and gain valuable feedback from which to create a more honed strategy.

Despite this, there are still many organisations that just want to tell their employees what they should be thinking and who will typically call in a consultant to advise them how to reach the stubborn elements of resistance within their firm! Such a policy is doomed to failure.

While it is often said that all staff are salespeople and front line for the business, it is normal for specific people to be the ones who spend a greater amount of their time talking to customers. They have an opportunity to see how customer relations and service could be improved. Feedback from these people is essential and a non-confrontational feedback system can give the company the information it needs to improve matters.

Shhh! Keep It Quiet

Sometimes it is inevitable that for all the right reasons it is impossible for a company to keep all its stakeholder groups fully informed all the time. During a so-called quiet period prior to the announcement of company results, or during times of mergers and acquisition negotiations, a company is banned by law from revealing information; and this can cause problems unless handled in an overtly sensitive manner, as Roger White, Director of Corporate Affairs at PricewaterhouseCoopers, told us. In 1998, PriceWaterhouse merged with Coopers and Lybrand, creating a new international firm with some 40 sites around the UK alone.

We had a big launch both internally and externally on the day the merger happened. Everybody got a guide to the new corporate identity and we put a lot of effort into communicating the fact that this was a new firm and a new start with two great legacies, although this was all about a merger of equals. So there were some very positive messages that we were able to impart.

In reality, I think it was one of the most successful mergers that I've ever seen or had any dealings with. Part of that is that we had an eight-month period between when the merger was announced and when it was finalised. During that time we put a lot of effort into communicating with our staff, saying, 'This is what it's about, this is what's going to happen, we're complimentary in these areas . . .' People had a real sense of what the new firm was going to be.

When we launched on the first day, we had big celebrations and in London there were open invitations to go from one building to another for drinks and all that sort of stuff, to make people feel that although it was all new they weren't losing anything.

We had to keep our clients and we had to keep our people during the process of the merger and I think in that time we only lost one client who blamed it on the merger. Staff turnover was at the lowest level that it had been in the previous five years. During periods of mergers or acquisitions, people usually expect there to be some job losses, so we were expecting to lose people even though we had said there wouldn't be any job losses because this merger was about growth and we needed them.

So people were waiting because they could see that this was a great opportunity. That was down in part to us pumping out regular communications even when we couldn't tell people very much. We would tell them, 'This is where we've got to with Brussels', or 'With the regulator the next landmark is this'; people felt they knew what was happening even if they didn't, because we communicated with them. But also we were able to paint a picture of what life was going to be like.

If you compare that with the IPO [initial public offering] we're going through now, an obvious difference is that during the merger we were able to tell people what to look forward to, whereas during an IPO with all the restrictions on what you can say, we can't do that. It's a much tougher environment.

Now obviously we've done a lot to explain to people what the rules are in relation to an IPO, so what we're trying to do is to adopt the same philosophy as when we went through the merger, and tell people what the process is. And we keep reinforcing that by telling them that we can't tell them anything, but that this is where we've got to and the timetable as it currently stands.

One of the lessons we learned during the merger was the need to listen, respond and react, and it was one of the things that I think we did very successfully. It's one of the reasons the merger went as well as it did. We had regular research projects going on and we were getting client feedback, as well as staff feedback, and we were monitoring the press because there was a small group of very influential journalists who write about us all the time and some of our people jest that if they haven't read it in the FT first they don't believe it!

As well as seeing what the journalists were writing, it was important to get some research into what they were thinking. It was the same with clients. We were able to identify a group of clients who had reservations about the merger – about it reducing choice and things like that – and it was important to make sure we were able to address those concerns, both to the clients themselves but also when we were talking to the regulators. I think probably the biggest single factor in the success in our communications during the merger was this programme of research, which we ran almost from day one when the deal was announced.

Making people aware of what is going on without speculation is not easy. If the company is going through a quiet period or some other change we suggest the following:

- Tell all employees the reason why you cannot communicate all the details of what is going on – and how long that situation might last.
- Give regular cascades of information – even if you cannot give any details.
- Ask them for feedback so that you can scotch any rumours before they get out of hand.

Causes of Ineffective Communications

A question for you to consider: What is the best way to create circumstances in which the culture, the team spirit and the environment all act to foster the motivation, initiative and creative juices of your people?

Attitudes in the workplace have changed dramatically over the past few decades. Internal communications itself has metamorphosed to a state that would be barely recognisable to an internal communications manager – had such a post existed – a couple of decades ago. It is not just that technology has advanced rapidly. The changing patterns of life and the workplace have, in many ways, forced the pace of change, demanding that the old condescending attitudes of the management – exemplified by the 'good news' company newsletter – are wholly inappropriate for the needs of today.

The changes did not happen overnight. The attitude that employees were purely effective pairs of hands to be 'managed' gave way gradually to the realisation that by treating them as mushrooms – by keeping them in the dark about what they were there for and what was trying to be achieved – was not the best way to help them to do their jobs well and by extension, not the best thing for the company either. Internal communications began, therefore, to focus on what to do and the best way of doing it. Personnel managers, as they were then regarded, got sucked into the process of communication, and training became the buzzword of the 1970s.

To the 'what' and the 'how' was soon added the 'why'. If employees understand why they are carrying out a particular task, reason dictates that they will work better when they have a purpose.

With hindsight that was all, perhaps, pretty obvious. Yet many directors still find that however much they inform their employees about what the company is trying to achieve, and however much they rabbit on about the mission values and the sales targets and the whys and the wherefores, their staff still lack the desired commitment, the 'buy-in' that they had hoped for. So what is going wrong? Or are directors expecting too much of their workforce?

Sadly, considering that the Industrial Revolution has been with us for a couple of centuries, properly structured employee communications is a relatively new art. In essence a purely top-down information flow is a hangover from the management control styles of the past. Obviously any company needs a unifying vision, with clearly defined goals and strong motivational messages thrown in for good measure. But to bring out the best in the workforce, a lateral exchange of ideas is also essential.

Bottom-up contributions of views not only ensure that suggestions for improving a process come from the very people who have to carry out that task every day – the very experts in that particular field – but they also go a long way to giving employees a better sense of self-worth, of encouraging them to believe that they have an important role to play in the overall profitability of the company, and ultimately lead to better motivation all round.

Understanding the rationale behind a director's pronouncements is all very well; but over-reliance on communications as a stream of verbal and visual messages only goes part-way in getting the real messages across. Changes in behaviour are also key to the new look workplace. Involvement has taken on a new meaning and in many ways is just as important as understanding.

When employees are told what is going on and upper management show they care about their staff, then mutual trust grows and people feel more involved with the aims of the company. Cries of 'They don't need to know that' or 'What's the point of telling them?' are merely an indication of a management culture that could be summed up by a much simpler sentence – 'I can't be bothered.' Directors cannot simply demand the loyalty of their staff. Loyalty has to be earned. When staff feel more involved, they work better and stay longer; and that, in short, is more likely to lay the groundwork for a successful company. Communications is a two-way street.

In a way it can all be likened to the institution of marriage. Boy meets girl; they start going out together; they decide to live together; after a couple of years and with pressure from their respective parents they decide to get married; there's a great big wedding and that is followed by an unforgettable honeymoon; they come back all elated. Then it's time to go back to work again and very soon they realise that nothing in particular has changed. True, they have a piece of paper to show they have tied the knot and, true, they both have a ring to show off to their friends; but now that the razzmatazz has died down what has actually changed?

Just as in that marriage, all too often employees come away from the great big company bash – that ever-so-expensive communications exercise in which directors extol the virtues of the company and exhort their staff to move on to ever greater and loftier plains – asking themselves, 'So what do I do that's different now?'

If that has ever happened in your company then, in short, your communications have failed. They have been purely media-led rather than getting translated into people's behavioural changes; because, despite all the grand sounding words being spoken at all the right times and at all the right opportunities, it is imperative that the actions of senior staff need to be aligned with the stated goals and values of the company.

'Don't do as I do; do as I say!' is a philosophy that has absolutely no place in the organisation of today if motivation and performance is to be enhanced. For how can junior employees be expected to live by the company's stated values if they perceive a lack of consistency with those values as practised by their supervisors, by the senior management, by the directors and, not least, by the chief executive himself? Attitudes are, after all, formed by experience as well as communications.

And if your people are not involved in the actual process of change, how can they be expected to feel an involvement and belief that things are really changing? It can be an unnerving experience for the control-minded manager – even more so for a director who has worked their way up from the bottom – to involve staff in the decision-making process, but it does in fact create decision-making at its most efficient.

By truly empowering their employees, directors soon find that it is, in reality, one of the best ways of unleashing their initiative and energy, not to mention a high level of personal commitment. The flip-side of that is aptly named 'negative power'. If employees are not given the authority and responsibility to help make things happen, it is all too easy for them to find 101 reasons why something cannot be done.

Perhaps one way of looking at it all is to treat it as an issue of identity. How staff interact with one another and how they deal with outsiders is reflected in their face-to-face contact with customers. When all your people live up to (or fail to live up to) the company's internal culture, customers really do notice.

Interestingly enough, the fact that so many UK companies are micro-sized – some 85% have fewer than five employees – is often responsible for a breakdown in good communication. Many make the false assumption that with so few staff, communication comes naturally and that company messages and values are picked up by a kind of osmosis.

And so they are in some companies; yet one of the main reasons for the failure to communicate is the lack of time faced by busy executives and employees who are so busy rushing about that they assume that others will know instinctively, or by observation, what they are thinking and doing.

Yet, one thing those micro-companies have on their side is informality. With up to around 15 employees, communications can still succeed while being informal, whereas above that number there needs to be a planned and structured formal communication too. At around 100 employees there is another break point where a structured employee communication programme becomes a necessity.

Of course, while communication is invaluable, it rarely achieves immediate results and it therefore needs to be 'nurtured' in order to build up trust and empathy over a period of time. Unfortunately, all too often, companies effectively put the cart before the horse. Theory would dictate that a director should in the first place want to communicate a message; he would then work out what he actually wanted to communicate and only then would he work out the best way of communicating it.

All too often, though, companies start the other way round. You might be amazed – or perhaps you might not be – how many firms decide to purchase an elaborate intranet system or start up a company newsletter and only then think about what it is they wish to say. Yet for any employee communication strategy to succeed, there has to be a firm commitment from the board itself to the purpose and demands of that strategy, and that commitment needs to be clearly stated. Failure to do so invariably leads to a dispirited workforce, who have had their expectations raised, only to find them dashed some months later.

Just as important as the 'what' and the 'why' questions are the 'when' and 'to whom' questions. The answer might seem self-evident; yet in practice one of the golden rules of communication is broken almost daily. Whenever possible, the workforce should always be the first to know. Much of the industrial unrest in the Britain of the 1970s and 1980s – when the UK situation earned for itself the epithet of 'the British disease' – could be traced to this one fundamental flaw in British management.

When the staff hear that the company is to be taken over, or that there are to be forced redundancies, or that there is good news and that a new factory is to be built or whatever it may be, just imagine how demoralising it must be for the employees to hear the news from the media – news that will have a direct impact on their lives. News that is second- or third-hand will always be mutilated in some way. (Remember the games of Chinese whispers in our former days?) The mitigating factors for a bad announcement may be given a lesser importance, or worse still, left out altogether. The context may not even be fully explained.

Naturally there are times when confidentiality demands that delicate information cannot be released early; but in that case the employees should always be told at the same time as the official announcement is made. Lack of information is the number one breeding ground for rumour and, once started on its rollercoaster ride, it is very difficult to apply the breaks to this vehicle of non-information. Staff rattled by rumour are not going to welcome glossy promises either. They will want the facts, and want them straight.

So just what are the main barriers to effective communication? For a start, many would argue that people in general are far too optimistic about the accuracy of the communication process. Communication skills tend to be taken for granted and a lack of such skills is far more easily recognised in others than in oneself.

How often have you seen a company director being interviewed on the television, floundering about, searching not just for the right word, but being sidetracked from giving out a clear and simple message by a not-very-experienced interviewer trying to make a name for himself? Verbal communication is just as much about listening as speaking and it is unfortunate that with many people, listening does not come naturally. Yet, if everyone concentrates on imparting information, who will be left to receive all the messages?

To gather and then keep everyone behind the arrowhead, communication must precede change and continue throughout it if hiatus and disaffection are not to occur. Thought, discussion and planning must include a healthy dose of reality.

The Cultural Divide

We all smile about the fact that the USA and Britain are two nations divided by a common language; but there are other cultural emphases as well as different meanings attributed to different words that can trip up the unwary who are lulled into a false sense of security by the apparent ease of having the common language. Actually, with so many imported television programmes, films and books permeating throughout our culture we all think that we understand perfectly what the 'other side' means and it can sometimes come as quite a nasty shock to discover that what we understood is totally the opposite of what was meant.

We had a graphic personal experience of this when we were doing some work for an American company based in California. In order to achieve as much as possible, as well as to enable their business to continue uninterrupted as much as possible, we arranged to go into the office both before and after their scheduled working day. We therefore appeared at 7.30 a.m. and were happy to burn the midnight oil with them too.

For a major part of the work we needed access to their offices at a time when they would not be there. So we lighted on the fact that they had an evening staff meeting beginning at 9 p.m. on the following Wednesday. We arranged to arrive at around 8.30 p.m. so that no time was lost.

At 10 p.m. we were asked if we would like coffee and cake and also to join the staff meeting where the directors were handing out accolades to the high achievers. We were formally introduced to the staff and then the office manager made an announcement. 'We know you guys are Brits, but you were obviously born the wrong side of the "pond" because you know how to work!' Was this a back-handed compliment or is it still a hangover from the 1970s and 1980s?

She went on to award us a golden-coloured railroad nail and said, 'I collected this nail off a disused railroad track in Chicago and painted it "Cadillac Gold". We'd like to give you this because you two have come all the way over here to nail our problem.' Accolades of this nature may seem over the top and possibly worthless in intrinsic terms. But we still have that railroad nail proudly displayed in our office for all to see. Saying 'thank you' is one of the most important of all communication tools.

Many British people find that American companies are much more direct in their communications than they are. You really know where you stand in a US company and have a sporting chance to change anything that doesn't fit, whereas there is a greater chance in a British company that the knife will be between your shoulder blades before you realise anything is wrong!

The US way may appear more brutal to us but, in the end, most people would rather know where they stand even if it were slightly more uncomfortable at first.

Of course, US and European labour laws are very different and both reflect and dictate cultural attitudes. If you have a takeover or a merger/acquisition, the USA would expect to have the whole thing wrapped up in about 30 days. If you went to Germany, Italy or France and said that, they'd think you were mad. You won't even get the ink dry on your initial intentions and letters to the unions within 30 days!

So the Americans are more direct and can be regarded as a bit brutal in the way they give information but they don't have the time to hang about and sugarcoat the pill too much. It takes time to assimilate a different culture and to be a viable part of it.

Remember, though, that many companies nowadays are multi-national and the communications in these companies tend to be a reflection of the culture within the company rather than the culture of the country in which it is operating. It is almost as if they are becoming nation states in their own right and the 'influence' of the company culture is greater, in general, than the influence of the local country culture – at least in terms of managing an organisation.

How Good a Communicator Are You?

Many directors live with a firm belief that whenever they talk to someone, they have effectively communicated a message to the recipient. Are you one of these people?

Whether you are or you're not, you might like to have a go at this standard exercise, regularly carried out by psychology under-graduates. Invite into your office a group of your staff and sit with your back to them, facing a wall. You will already have given each a pencil and sheet of paper and on your lap will be a diagram made up of rectangles all of equal size. All angles will be either 45° or 90°. All rectangles touch either at the corners or midpoints of the sides. (See Figure 3.2)

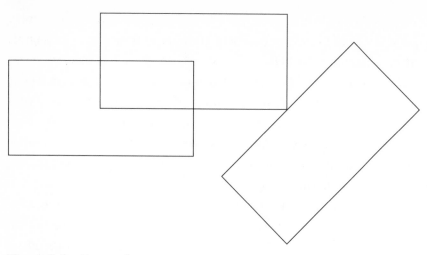

Figure 3.2 *Rectangles*

Now, try explaining to them using purely verbal instructions how to draw the diagram themselves. You might just be surprised how few of them get the finished drawing correct in every respect. Using a similar diagram, face the staff and as they draw allow them unlimited opportunity to ask you questions. Although the process takes longer, the resulting accuracy will be much higher. Scientists call this cybernetics system 'negative feedback' – using an error message to reduce the level of the original error so that the end result is an error-free product.

Perhaps, to sum up, the principles of good communication can be encapsulated in that entreaty, 'Do unto others as you would have them do unto you.' In other words, consider how you would want to receive messages rather than how you would impart them; think how you might react to someone else giving you the particular message you want to give out yourself; and when you have considered all the pros and cons, turn the situation on its head and impart your message in the way you know will be received in the best possible way.

But remember, in this age of hi-tech gadgetry and fast computer systems nothing comes close to having a quiet word in someone's ear. Meeting people face to face and building relationships cannot be substituted by technology alone. And in an age when more seems to be expected from fewer people with less expenditure, one of the most valuable – perhaps the most valuable – message to communicate (as we have already noted) can be summed up in two simple words: 'Thank you.'

FOUR

SWOT Analysis

If ever you needed convincing of the effectiveness of a communications programme – internal or external – you couldn't do better than to use the well-established method of the SWOT analysis. Not only does it enable you to focus on the Strengths, Weaknesses, Opportunities and Threats of all your communications, but it is also a clear guide to the validity, value and awareness of growing and improving your interaction and feedback with your different audiences.

If we concentrate on some of the internal points raised in a SWOT analysis, the same principles can be applied to the more familiar external communications. People, after all, tend to spend more time on their external communications than they do internally. (The same principle can also be applied to the ways and means of effecting your communications.)

Strengths

Not surprisingly, the whole practice of *internal* communications and marketing can be based on the well-established model of *external* marketing. The same principles are easily translated into the world of the internal market, identifying the staff as your internal customers.

This translation of these accepted principles from external to internal marketplace makes the inception of proactive internal communications more readily acceptable as it does away with the need to introduce something totally new. People, after all, are often fearful of new things, be they processes or practices, because of the learning curve, which has to be overcome and achieved. There is also the added threat of the performance required from the management and general leadership within a firm.

So, pulling in to the internal marketplace the familiar terminology and focus areas used in the external marketplace – such as target markets, products, promotion and price – should in theory prove a great deal less threatening and become a strength. Use of these familiar terms also enables the vision of the employees to be embraced and helps to overcome some tricky areas and barriers, which any new plans are liable to throw up.

If this approach is taken, then each division, team and individual will see the benefits of a change in perspective and the values that are put upon them. If employees are treated as internal customers then they feel important to the organisation as individuals, teams and divisions, and the whole organisation gains strength from this.

This change of attitude will enhance the internal services provided, as well as encouraging commitment to the introduction of the change process. In turn, individual and team creativity will become much more proactive and as a result the movement for comprehensive, multifaceted internal communications will actually speed up, as the vision of a potentially more vibrant and effective organisation becomes widely appreciated.

When you stop to think about it, it really is quite strange that some employers often dislike the fact that their people, who are meant to be at work, stop and talk to one another. And yet surely it is vital to any organisation – be it household, village, business or multinational – that people should not just get talking with one another, but that they should positively gossip!

Without gossip, no group of people can work well as a team. When people do gossip and talking is encouraged between teams, then improvements in products, methodology, services and high quality become the norm. In effect, the 'that will do' philosophy gets consigned to history.

Once you have engendered a general acceptance of this change in focus, and more effort, money and training is invested in the business of communication, it will be easier to gain the co-operation of those people who traditionally bridle at receiving top-down instruction. Admittedly it takes more time giving your people more involvement, yet you might be surprised by how much it can generate quite astonishing results.

In exactly the same way as can be seen with external markets, the energy produced by this involvement process positively encourages commitment and motivation to the services and products provided – and that includes your 'internal customers'. The process is the same – it is only the target market that is different. In the same way, it is essential to take the same care over the database detail as one would with the external marketing database, as this will endorse the organisation's commitment to its people – your 'internal customers'.

Indeed, the whole feeling of the organisation and its internal relationships will be enhanced because of the focus on the need for contribution by individuals and the retention of good, workable relationships. The 'internal customer' has needs, just as much as you do, and those will be of prime importance in the overall process of internal communications. This in turn leads on to a better targeting of your external market as the mindset achieved by a change of attitudes creates a focus on multidirectional and multilayered communications. The improved services, support and products, which will follow, will be a natural by-product of a greater cohesion within your team. In addition, you will have better informed and motivated people who will not need to be incentivised just to work.

Most organisations of any size have a strong brand image – whether this be of service or product – and the same brand loyalty and wholehearted acceptance is achievable within the organisation as well as outside it. These brand images are assets on the balance sheet and, together with the people who make up the organisation, these will form a stronger branded image and asset value, which will soon also make an appearance on the financial statements.

The seamless cohesion of an organisation that practises good internal communications achieves more than just good talk. There is a high price to be paid by organisations that do not subscribe wholeheartedly to the practice: that of slippage in delivery, shortfalls, substandard work and sticking-plaster attempts to rein in the problems.

And so we come to what must be the greatest advantage you will have over any organisation or competitor who does not comprehensively implement good multidirectional internal marketing philosophies, interactive communications and practice; your organisation will have an inner intrinsic strength beyond that of others, which will stumble and crumble into factions as disparate divisions or departments wrangle internally with one another. The cost is theirs; the advantage yours!

Weaknesses

The biggest problem that any organisation has in coming to terms with the attitudinal shift made necessary by the introduction of multidirectional internal communications is that of the middle layers of management. Since the late 1980s, many layers have gone, or at least been threatened by, downsizing, and so-called business process re-engineering. Observations and market research show that middle management generally tend to try to control information in order to protect their positions. They see their security and power in this control.

It is one of those unfortunate truisms that disinformation and mal-information, in either direction, are unwritten but well-understood middle-management tools for control. It really boils down to their perception that control equals management – at the very least of one's own personal fiefdom. In fact, good management has an essence of control but that control should be delegated within the responsibilities of each individual working for the organisation.

It is easy to see that the information sifting and blocking that goes on in middle management is wholly detrimental to an organisation but in practice it can be quite difficult to shift this middle-management mud. Control of information is, after all, a very powerful tool. People in this position are very defensive and need help in reassessing their sense of self-worth within a talking organisation. Resistance can be considerable and defensive behaviour costly in relationships and energy within the firm.

A genuine understanding of the situation of middle managers will enable the implementation to be more easily effected because potential resistance will be identified in the process. An emphasis on internal communications being an intrinsic part of your internal marketing may well reduce their defensiveness but you will have to ensure that their stranglehold on information – both up and down and throughout the hierarchy of the organisation – has to be broken for communications to succeed.

Planning, time and effort are therefore needed to enable such changes to happen effectively. In the same way that career development and the perception of career has changed considerably since the creation of flatter organisational structures, the 'security blanket' of controlling information flow and the perception of one's self-worth being dependent on it need to undergo a perceptional change.

In addition to the middle-management mud that can disable multi-directional communications, there are budget items that are always first to go when the business goes through a lean time, or budgets are cut. Marketing is usually the first budget to be questioned and training of any sort follows shortly after. Both of these, of course, are fundamental to the effectiveness of marketing and, by extension, to enable internal marketing to gather momentum with the time and money that are so necessary to an enhanced internal communications programme. It could so easily be considered that investing in good internal marketing and communications is a costly exercise that just panders to staff, who ought instead to think themselves lucky to have a job – any kind of job – in this day and age.

Organisations in the UK have, traditionally, been particularly lax in their investment in people – both in training and in treating them as if they really are people, rather than some sort of robot or automaton. It can be quite a challenge for an organisation's governing body to overcome the arguments that training people just enables them to leave and get more money elsewhere. Involving people in decisions on how work should be planned and achieved is sometimes taken as a sign of weakness in a manager – even if it does identify the best process and benefit the organisation far more. In this, lack of communication is often wrongly perceived to be control and retention of power.

So to reap the benefits of multiple communications, these arguments must be overcome. People are the most valuable assets of any company and investment in them through internal marketing will well repay the wariness of the board in deciding to change to this way of working. But it must be recognised that there is not a long tradition of internal marketing and communications in the UK and so there is a shortage of peer group colleagues to give the decision-makers a feeling of comfort in deciding to implement such good practice.

The high profile nature of the internal market, together with the fact that the channels for distribution are the people within an organisation, makes it potentially one of high risk. And so the communication of an attitudinal shift in the philosophy of the organisation must be communicated to gain the co-operation of all the people; and all of the services, information and products have to move through this channel.

The complementary roles of corporate affairs and human resources, together with the rest of the board, have to be softened so that the internal media carry the messages effectively and without upset. The choice of which media should be used – intranet, video conferencing, conference call, e-mail, fax, talk, meetings, newsletters, phone, memos, etc. – has to be sensitively made.

To make it really work well, trainers have to be updated and as a consequence high quality trainers will produce the excellence needed. In the UK, organisations, have neglected training for too long a time. So your plan needs to start with training the trainers and ensuring that they have the richness of knowledge and experience needed to engender confidence in those being trained. It will be no good at all – in fact, it could even be more damaging – to use a trainer who does not inspire confidence and who does not have the stature to generate such confidence in a receptive audience.

The long-term vision of the payback and reward of implementing comprehensive internal marketing and two-way communications will be able to be understood but there will be misgivings from people who will not be able to see how they, with their already full schedules, can find the time that will be necessary to spend for the commitment needed. And to make matters worse, there is no easy way to quantify effectiveness, just as it is also difficult to prove the bottom-line benefits, as is often the case with marketing and public relations.

As there is now generally a greater awareness of communications in the management of change, and the roles of all marketing and public relations also involve embracing change in proactive roles for the future, there should be fewer people who are nowadays fearful of the discipline needed in changing to multidirectional internal communications. But be aware that there *will* be fear and distrust of the change.

Opportunities

In the 1990s, many organisations became steeped in the philosophy of total quality and this, therefore, presented a wonderful opportunity to put over the idea of the internal market. Indeed, there is nowadays a much greater likelihood of acceptance of the concept since the downsizing and flattening of organisational structures. Since there is also more technology-driven change occurring, there is a greater expectation of the need to absorb new ideas and of the need for change. Of course, so as not to overwhelm people, the learning curve must be carefully planned with plenty of space around it for reflection.

Along with embracing the new technology that enables more businesses to become yet more effective, there is a great opportunity of advantage over competitors through dynamic multidirectional internal communications as part of internal marketing.

Threats

Threats only apply to an organisation that rejects the implementation of good internal communications and does not regard its people as its own internal market; for it is the dynamism of committed people that generates energy and improvement in service and product quality. That change and energy will percolate throughout the organisation. This means that people who think 'That will do' about a piece of work will never improve the quality of their work and this leads to the danger of another external customer being not quite satisfied.

Energy generates energy. You know that's true and your customers are attracted by the awareness shown by enthusiastic and committed people where they know they will get a better service. A management that is constantly dealing with customer complaints is always in crisis-management mode and this is hardly likely to enable any opportunity to implement good practice. This in turn leads to a loss of morale.

An organisation that does not grasp opportunities lacks hope and, in turn, its people lack hope and expectations of better things. The internal feel-good factor is very powerful and if diminished or extinguished it imposes a great threat to the organisation concerned.

The impact of non-motivated or only partly motivated employees is enormous and the cost to the organisation and the financial bottom line can be considerable. If the company is failing to market itself internally and failing to communicate, then its people assess their own worth in relation to their work and tend to leave. The cost of loss of unmotivated staff can be enormous, but it is avoidable if the right communications about the right services and internal products are made in the right way.

We all know the damage that uncommitted employees who stay on, despite their unhappiness, can do. These disaffected people have, in effect, left the organisation but they choose to stay only on the basis of collecting their pay cheque. Their lack of motivation is infectious and creates apathy, if not negative attitudes in others. This in turn leads to a reduction in the suggestions and improvements that people make in order to be innovative and also a distancing of employees from the products and services they are providing externally. Such organisations in essence loose their hearts and minds.

These negative effects create a puddingy and phlegmatic attitude, which makes it far harder for the board to reach the external customer – and for the external customer to reach the board. Workers in this situation make it almost impossible to implement or take advantage of any innovative moves and their organisations suffer accordingly.

There are also threats to an organisation that decides to go for full implementation of an internal marketing strategy. It is not something that can be done as a half-measure. Within the organisation, the struggle for power can be the most powerful threat to the implementation of multidirectional, internal communications and the internal market.

The *only* way to overcome this is to involve all of your people and to win their hearts and minds to the concept. You cannot implement it top-down, as this is a contradiction in terms. It cannot be implemented by management who suddenly decide to leave their ivory towers and wander about saying hello to staff, in whom they have taken little or no interest before. It can only be done by involving the whole organisation and approaching it as a whole organisation; opening up the channels of communication and removing the fears. All in all, these fears have to be replaced with hope, aspirations and, above all, goodwill. The communication has to say what it means.

For a best practice and highly practical SWOT analysis of external or internal communications, as well as the ways and means of communicating and analysing the roles of those who should be attributed as the messengers of particular information, your blueprint can be built after considering these points:

- Map out who should give input and get agreement that they should be there.
- Get everyone who should be involved to the discussion.
- Allocate enough time for people to be free to throw ideas into the pot.
- Talk through and think through the ideas before discarding any – however apparently wild they may appear.
- Make sure there are no interruptions to spoil the flow.
- Give people a break before you sieve the ideas down with them.
- Focus and bring a sense of reality to what might have started out as a totally off-the-wall idea.
- String together a skeleton of the outcome for your communication plan.

FIVE

External Audiences

___

When planning an external communications strategy, in the same way as you did with your internal communications, you have to truly identify all your audiences before you can even begin to think about what it is you wish to get across to them. Not all audiences will require the same information, or even require it in the same format. So before you even start on that track you need to work out in very simple terms:

- What are we trying to say?
- Why?
- To whom?
- How?

Many people are so anxious to get talking that they don't think about what the potential recipient might want to know.

We always start by drawing a communications map so that nobody gets forgotten and this visually highlights the relationship between these groups; the relationship between the messages then follows on. Obviously the map will change from company to company. The aide mémoire in Figure 5.1 is simply that and should be used while you think through all the external audiences (and their agendas) with whom you need to communicate.

Customers and Clients

Business success depends upon customers. And since the advent of the Internet and other technologies, never have real customer communications been more important. Fifty years ago in the austerity

Figure 5.1   *External communications*

years following the war, most people were satisfied if their products simply worked. Choice wasn't really an issue and service wasn't something that the Brits were famous for! It was a sellers' market through and through. Purchasing was more often made on the basis of need rather than want.

But everything has been turned on its head as companies have grown larger and become more global. Increasing competition and a rise in customer expectations means that today's company cannot ignore the need to communicate brilliantly with its customers or it will simply die. Why should a prospective customer bother with you if your main competitors are only too happy to communicate with them and you're not?

'Enlightened' companies of yesteryear were good at basic customer care solutions such as training their receptionists to be courteous and helpful. Today's organisation needs to concentrate on marketing communications as well as providing customer service and aftercare in a way that will retain those customers in the long term. Here traditional customer relationship management (CRM) techniques are important. Poor service, a lack of understanding of customer needs and arrogance on the part of the organisation are usually listed as the main reasons that customers become one-off and do not come back for more, rather than just on price alone.

Marketing communications cover many different areas, from deciding who prospective customers are in the first place – as well as their needs and desires – to letting them know what products are available.

Measuring Opinion

Measuring opinion is a crucial part of building an appropriate or successful communication plan. Not only is communication a two-way process but a company that gets genuine feedback from its customers and target groups will be better-equipped to know how to impart its own messages.

So consumer surveys and questionnaires are widely used to garner the views of prospective customers because they are cheap and easy to organise and can give useful information on the demographics of the different marketplaces. The trouble is, they tend not to be very accurate because they tend to deal in generalities, they take little account of people's perceptions and many people will proffer the answers they feel are 'wanted' by the surveyor. However, they can be used for identifying trends and for getting a 'broadbrush' picture in order to identify areas for more in-depth and specific research, which can then be undertaken in a more specialised and focused way.

Often, the next stage is to set up focus groups, which can provide subjective and objective information as well as allowing customers to get involved in the decision-making process. Here the composition of the groups is of paramount importance and typically eight to ten participants will be an optimum number. A relaxed environment is essential to encourage open discussion, and a facilitator who is experienced in chairing such meetings is necessary to keep the group focused. Then the resultant reports and data can prove to be extremely useful in honing the communication plan and promotional activities.

Promotional Communications

Promoting your goods and services can include a wide variety of activities in gaining the attention of your prospective clients. Advertising, public relations, events, direct mail and even the packaging of the goods themselves say a lot about your company and its products. All play an important part in the communications and marketing mix, building your brand and gaining your market share as well as letting people know what you as a company stand for.

Promotional activities in the main are all about tempting your prospects by creating a feeling of excitement about your products or services or a feeling of belonging to a tribe, which is associated with your company. There is always a strong temptation when communicating the positives to overplay the benefits that a prospect will get, but exaggeration is something that has a terrible habit of coming back to haunt you in later times. Advertising standards bodies have their role to play in stopping unsustainable claims, but customers want what they have been promised, and if they have been misled into the benefits they will receive, they will always hold you responsible for non-delivery.

This is something that advertising professionals must always weigh in the balance. On the one hand, they want their products to stand out from the competition; on the other, their marketing flair should not verge on false claims and promises. Clarity, courtesy and conciseness should all be elements of the marketer's armoury, but in addition they should concentrate on cultivating feelings of sincerity, approachability, humour, tact and enthusiasm to weigh in with the written and spoken messages already communicated.

When the airline industry was assailed by the success of EasyJet and Ryanair, many major airlines decided to meet this challenge head-on with their own look-alikes. British Airways spawned Go!, KLM started

Buzz, Virgin began Virgin Express, and so on. It will be interesting to see whether the effect these low-cost carriers have on the industry is similar to that which Direct Line had on the established insurers.

But now some of the established airlines, who saw this offshoot as a means to retain market share during bad times, and while reinventing themselves, have found that the venture has backfired to the extent that Go! was even advertising against British Airways a year after it had been sold off.

Iain Burns, BA's General Manager of Corporate Communications, told us:

> Go! was BA's response to addressing the low-cost no-frills sector. It was a mistake. What it did was to freeze management into thinking that they had an answer for addressing their own cost problems.
>
> Out of Europe we were losing £300m a year. What was the answer? We have Go! now. But that doesn't address £300m-worth of loss on an annual basis. Selling it off did, because suddenly people couldn't say we had Go! anymore. With 20/20 hindsight it's something we now know we shouldn't have done, but we did. Setting up Go! was not an answer to BA's problems but actually created bigger problems as well as a smokescreen behind which to hide from the reality of those problems. Selling it was the only way that BA could have a clear view of their path to regaining their market position.
>
> We set it up at £25m and sold it for £100m but it caused confusion for the staff and it caused confusion for the customers as well and gave totally mixed messages. There's no airline that has successfully been able to mix the two. I'm not saying you can't do it, but it's our view that you can't do it successfully.

The much-publicised fiasco over the non-branded tail fins found on all BA's aircraft – which had been pushed through by their former Chief Executive Bob Ayling and subsequently dropped, while Virgin assumed the British persona of the Union Jack – caused BA an own-goal. In communication terms, an airline going from having an 'establishment' profile among the public and the City was giving very mixed messages about itself, and it is no wonder that it ceased to be the City's darling and the 'world's favourite airline'.

Apart from customers, businesses need to consider a number of other different audiences who can play a major part in the fortunes of a company. Be aware:

- Customers are becoming tyrants because of greater ability to choose more widely.
- Most customers want only to get good service and be told the truth about delivery, quality, terms and conditions, etc.
- And check all your small print. It may be legally right, but is it losing you sales because of its attitude?

Suppliers

The majority of businesses have to get their raw materials from an outside supplier and although traditional communications with suppliers have been on the basis of beating them down to the lowest possible supply price, this does not make for good long-term business relationships. This can produce a dichotomy of communications messages. The brief of most purchasing departments is to source supplies at the lowest possible price, and certainly in the public sector it is normal to go for the lowest tender, commensurate with delivery.

Put yourself in the shoes of your suppliers, however, and things begin to look a bit different. Sometimes good communications can save both sides time and money, and both parties can get what the Chinese are wont to call a 'happy contract' – one in which the basis of the contract is that neither party can walk away thinking that they have potentially been out-negotiated by the other party. In particular, many organisations could help their suppliers to anticipate their needs if only they would talk to them.

A perfect example of this occurred recently when a consultancy was called in to a manufacturing plant to identify ways of improving efficiency and profits. One of the processes they looked at involved the manufacturer in splicing and welding together lengths of wire – which had been delivered in 100 ft rolls – into 120 ft lengths. Their purchasing department had identified a supplier who could deliver this particular wire for a good price, but no one had thought to ask them if it would be possible to deliver the raw wire in lengths of 120 ft instead of the 100 ft lengths they traditionally supplied. The fact is that they could, and the slightly increased cost for custom-supplying 120 ft lengths was more than made up for in the savings of time and effort on behalf of the manufacturer. Both parties were the eventual winners by the simple expedient of talking to one another!

It is in every organisation's interests to have good relations with its suppliers, and this depends more than anything else on well-planned two-way communications. Successful communications in this area can play a major role in improving business performance.

Suppliers, as one of the stakeholder groups in a company, are often still treated in a less than friendly manner despite the company's dependency on their goodwill.

- Check your corporate mindset toward suppliers and amend your attitude if it is not going to be helpful in times of need.
- Try to see any problems from their point of view and communicate that you have understood them.

Owners and Shareholders

Regardless of how well a business is doing, it will have to keep its owners and shareholders well and truly informed of the current state of the organisation. Owners invariably start many of the communication processes by asking the board endless questions to which they want answers.

Shareholders tend to be either institutional or private, and although both need to be kept informed, it is necessary to communicate effectively with brokers, analysts and the financial press, especially – but not necessarily only – for larger companies. Some institutions, for instance, invest significantly in underperforming companies and will enforce change through the power of their shareholding where they deem it to be necessary. This can and regularly does include the shifting of what they see as underperforming executives – for the main reason that an institution decides to invest in a company is its perception of the qualities inherent in the company's high echelons of management.

'Ordinary' shareholders tend to be majorly influenced by the financial press and so any communications strategy ignores them at their peril. Larger companies often have a shareholder relationship manager whose sole job is to communicate with financial journalists, city analysts and major shareholders, establishing and keeping open communication channels to ensure they are fully informed, so that they will communicate on their findings to a larger audience in a fair light, and hopefully in a manner that will be informed rather than speculative.

In terms of importance, though, the top 30 investment institutions in the UK control about 40% of the British market and traditionally companies have relied on their brokers to communicate with these institutions. But with the increased competition for capital, the chief executive or one of his team is now making regular contact with fund managers.

Investment fund managers like consistent results, but they also want to know as much as possible about the nature of the business and about the quality of the management structure. Making sure that there is an open and vibrant communication channel with them can ensure that some of the more violent market fluctuations are not encountered. Perception is all in share dealing and investment, and excellent communications are essential if this positive perception is not to wane.

Most large companies have a core group of investors with whom they have a good working relationship and with whom they regularly communicate information. The real problem comes, though, in com-municating with peripheral fund managers since, if the core investors were to pull out of their shareholdings for any reason, the company would need to ensure that they could raise more shareholdings from these peripheral investors pretty quickly. Because this latter group have limited shareholdings – or even none at all – their direct contact with the company is likely to be pretty marginal; yet consistent support in the market is essential if a company is to raise further funding. So the conundrum is how to communicate effectively with this group, yet not to use up too much management time in so doing.

Another City group that has to be catered for is the stockbrokers' analysts. There are hundreds of analysts who report on individual sectors. Some are better than others, but in the main stockbrokers listen to their recommendations, even if some say 'sell' while others say 'buy' at the same time. But many fund managers rely on brokers' analysts to do the donkey-work, albeit that they are more likely to get the opinions from, say, three or more before acting on their recommendations.

Here, again, we have another problem. Because there are so many analysts competing for attention in the market, they tend to publish reams of analysis. Much of this is simply to generate press coverage for their own firms. But in the meantime it takes up a great deal of executive time, and many financial directors slough off this duty to specialist investor relations staff.

One of the complaints about the Enron collapse is that no one was warned that there was anything wrong before the collapse. But there's a practice among analysts that, if they want the investment bank business from big corporations, they have to give a positive stock rating masquerading as a technical advice. They feel that they are not able to recommend selling any shares if they want to do (or did do) business with that corporation. So they will use a phrase such as 'long-term buy' as a euphemism for 'sell' and people in the know understand what this means. This is another example of the codes professionals use to communicate with one another and their specialist audiences.

Although the influence of analysts on fund managers is great, the influence of national newspapers such as the *Financial Times* and the business pages of the other broadsheets cannot be minimised. Nowhere is this more important than when a negative article in the press suggests problems with a company, at which point the executive team may find themselves spending an inordinate amount of time carrying out damage limitation. Once such an article is printed in one newspaper, you can be as sure as eggs is eggs that another will pick it up and that analysts and brokers will hone in on the company to demand some answers pretty fast.

Negative articles also get stored in cuttings libraries, and one of the most difficult tasks for the financial communicator is then to ensure that such negative comments are placed in context and to ensure that the media are kept up to date with newer, more positive messages.

The financial performance of a company, however, can be only one aspect of a company's communications agenda and therefore it cannot be isolated from the rest of the communications and public relations functions of an organisation. The financial PR needs to tie in with the messages being put out by the corporate affairs and public relations departments, if these functions are split up – as they tend to be in many larger companies.

Indeed, if the financial communications function is outsourced to a specialist agency, then close contact with the in-house functions needs to be maintained. Some financial PR agencies are excellent at investor relations; some have better media contacts; some a better relationship with the City. Very few have excellent skill sets in all three areas. When choosing such an outside firm, it is important therefore to ask around and to see which firm has the skills you need; otherwise it can take a good six months' worth of fees before discovering that the firm you have picked doesn't have all the skills that you have identified as being necessary.

As well as financial PR agencies, there are also firms that deal purely with investor relations on behalf of their clients. Their brief is usually to identify the most appropriate investors for management visits, prepare executives for presentations, and brief fund managers and analysts.

Many, however, believe that outsourcing both financial PR and investor relations can lead to a murky overlap of competing functions between the two specialities. And in any case, some would argue that where the expertise lies in-house, then an in-house director is more likely to act within the corporate ethos than an outside consultant. This ignores the fact, of course, that having a fully fledged department in-house may not be cost effective – and that's even assuming that it has the expertise necessary.

Peter Waine of Hanson Green offers this advice for the board.

I would give the following guidelines about communicating with the City. First, it should only be the finance director and the CEO and maybe the chairman – at certain times.

The only time a non-exec should communicate with the City is if he really feels the company board is acting incorrectly and he hasn't been able to get the board's agreement. He must then say, 'Look, I'm going to go over your heads and appeal to the City.' It's very rare that they do that but there is a desperate need, on occasion. It would be seen as stabbing the company in the back but there are ways of doing it.

Communicating with the City is tricky at best and the best way to do it properly is either to employ the right people with the right experience or else to call in the professionals.

Corporate Affairs

We all work in a world dominated by regulations that have been imposed by some governmental or professional body. We may not like it, but most of these regulations are the rule of law and every business needs to comply with them. Many impose considerable costs on a business and it makes sense, therefore, for organisations to monitor them in their draft stages to try to influence the policy-makers before their ideas become law.

Larger companies can employ lobbyists on their behalf both to monitor and to put forward their views to the bureaucrats. Smaller businesses can use their collective membership of bodies such as the CBI, Federation of Small Businesses (FSB), chambers of commerce and professional institutes to represent them.

In addition, it is a good idea to keep your local member of parliament regularly informed of what your organisation is doing since they might not only represent your interests in Westminster, but also view you as the specialists in your particular field that they can approach when they need advice or to communicate on a particular issue. Most of the utility companies, for instance, have a regular programme of events set up for MPs and MEPs in their areas, since environmental matters are often high up on an MP's agenda and utility companies are often viewed as easy targets by environmental protesters.

- Take care when embarking on this kind of communication – it could be long and costly.
- It is an unfortunate fact that many MPs, MEPs, self-appointed champions and arbiters know little about running a business. Not only might they come out with fatuous comments but also they might expect you to provide them with reams of research material while they are on their learning curve. Sometimes, however, it is an inevitable cost of doing business in the real world.

Community Relations

Successfully communicating the values of a business in a local community is important in maintaining a reputation for being beneficial to that community, since the perceptions of the people who live and work in the vicinity of your business can play an important role when you are attempting, for instance, to get planning permission for expansion or when trying to recruit the right local staff.

Giving money to charities, although practised by many companies, doesn't go far enough, as many will interpret this as a corporate sop or conscience money. Instead, many larger firms actively encourage involvement in the community in some way. Some organisations second their staff to work in the locality on special community projects. Others actively support voluntary work or provide facilities for events.

Manchester Airport, for instance, took the decision to support the arts in the North West and regularly allows its facilities to be used for performances. They even have a full-time arts co-ordinator whose job is to ensure that the message that the airport is a full participating member of the local community is upheld. In this way they hope that negative publicity, which is invariably generated by something as intrusive as an airport, is minimised.

Indeed, many large companies make an effective bridge between themselves and the local community and improve the perception of themselves in the process. Take for instance local out-of-town super-markets – they want to sell their products off their shelves and to outsell their competitors. That's a nice simple objective but it needs to be packaged so that their customers see them as being friendly and helpful, while relieving them of their money as well. This seems on the face of it to be a very sceptical view but if you pare it down to the bare bones it is precisely what happens. So these supermarkets dream up schemes that generate loyalty towards themselves and rejection of their competition in a rather complex series of moves, which make emotional purchasing the norm.

For many years, Sainsbury's ran a scheme that donated £250 to each of a series of youth organisations every year. Sometimes this was £250 per store and sometimes £250 per geographical grouping of stores. There was a four-year rotation based mainly on the age of the target groups, whereby the focus was on playgroups, mother and toddler groups and the like, with one year focusing on disability groups of every age and another on teenage groups. The whole basis of the take-up of the scheme was the perceived benefit to a group of children or young people of a cash donation, which was to purchase equipment for them.

The general public saw posters in the local store and applied through the store management, making an impassioned case as to why their chosen group should be selected. Sainsbury's head office charities department always had the final say as to who received the donation and the local branch manager made the presentation with a photo opportunity bursting with happy children and bits of equip-ment, which would appeal to the local press and sell more papers too.

So everyone was happy; children celebrated, parents thought the supermarket was helpful and the cost of all this touchy-feely publicity and increased loyalty was very low indeed.

HSBC always sponsors Young Enterprise – the national programme of getting schoolchildren to set up and run a small business for a year – and their local bank managers get involved in the advice and mentoring to the competing teams. After all, where will those individuals go when they want to open their own bank accounts?

Tesco has its promotions with computers-for-schools vouchers, which are collected avidly during their open season. The scheme, which started with the now-defunct Acorn computers, offers computing equipment and books to local schools who then have to collate and log all the vouchers and apply for their goodies. You have to collect an awful lot of vouchers to get a computer, but the feeling that Tesco's is there to help the community is a very strong motivation toward purchasing from them.

These schemes work if they catch the public imagination. And they can be great fun too. The essence, though, is for the company to be seen to be putting something back into the community and being magnanimous about it.

Before embarking on a community relations programme:

- Think through your parameters.
- Calculate how much time as well as money you want to devote to it.
- Get your people to nominate prospective charities for adoption by the company.
- Appoint a member of staff as the main point of contact for all outside communications.
- Appraise the potential recipients to ensure their involvement is good for your profile.
- Be realistic and try to choose a programme that has good photo opportunities.
- Make sure you tell the world at large about it – locally, regionally and nationally.

The Media

Public relations and marketing fill numerous volumes in their own account. Suffice it to say that good media relations are critical for any business and play a significant role in the fortunes of any company.

Peter Waine at Hanson Green believes that boards are sometimes very bad at communicating with the press.

Often the press have to guess at the story and read between the lines. Companies are often too confidential about things but I do think that a lot of companies don't know how much information is appropriate or whether sometimes they swamp the journalists or whether they give too little. It is difficult but many businesses make a difficult task seem impossible – and it's not.

Roger White, Director of Corporate Affairs at Pricewaterhouse Coopers, believes that having good relationships with journalists is paramount.

There is a group of journalists who write about us as a business. And we know them well and have good relationships with them, even when they write something we don't like. It's our policy to have good relationships with them since we have to work together and they're only doing their jobs. It's much more sensible for both sides if we can work together. I'm not averse to having a row with a journalist when I think they have written something that I think is wrong. If, however, they write something that is right but I don't like it, or my bosses don't like it, then I'm afraid that's a fact of life. If you think there are any misinterpretations then you try to get them to see your perspective on things.

Part of the job of my PR team, I always tell them, is to be the intermediaries between our people here and the journalists out there. We have brilliant people here who are real technicians and, like all brilliant technicians, they get into jargon. Part of the job of my team is to interpret that and present it to the outside world.

Depending on what it is, basically the rule is that nobody talks to the press without talking to me or my team. People are empowered to talk to the press on their areas of expertise, but everyone knows that when it is a corporate issue then it's me or my head of PR who act as corporate spokesmen. When I first came in to this firm 11 years ago we didn't have those disciplines and structures in place, but the successful side of things has helped to build the process as much as dealing with the problems. It's all too easy in an organisation of our size to give a whole load of conflicting messages, so we try to ensure that everybody has a lot of freedom, but only within their own specialist areas and where they are comfortable to talk.

Identifying the right journalists to speak to for any story is as crucial as identifying your audiences in the first place. Take a typical day in British Airways' communications HQ, for example. Iain Burns, General Manager of British Airways' Corporate Communications:

When we have a communications piece of work to do – say a big piece on where BA's moving to in the future – I'll get my team around me and we'll think and look at all the communications. The obvious targets are Fleet Street and staff. We'll also have someone around the table from this department looking at the travel trade, someone looking at government, someone at the local community (what impact does it have in, say, Belfast for example) and then they will work locally with the people in the government affairs department, the people who are in sales who are talking with the travel trade, and so on. We just look at all the constituent audiences and then each of these people will go off and talk with our specialist internal audiences who are dealing with them. With government affairs, of course, they are talking not just with Westminster but with Brussels, Washington and whoever as well.

Now, this department has what is called a 'news desk' – that's the press office; all it does is react, react, react . . . 63 000 calls a year. Then I have a team that I call 'operations' and that's what I think most people see as an airline – cabin crew, the planes and the staff out in the airports. They deal with external and internal communications. So they're all account managers.

I have people dealing with commercial and international

on the proactive marketing side of the business and all the agencies overseas; I have a big team in America, our biggest market; there's a head of internal channels that looks after the intranet and the newspaper, and someone who does corporate work – finance and legal etc. It used to be 99 people, but following 11 September it's being reduced to 53. So it's a large department.

I also use agencies – financial, of course, but I also use one for covering Europe, another in Cyprus that looks after the Mediterranean and CIS [Commonwealth of Independent States] countries, and different agencies down in Asia and the Far East. But obviously agencies have to bring in added value. If they don't I won't hire them.

Roger White fully concurs with this view.

I don't think agencies can ever get close enough to the story to understand your business. The good ones can get a little bit under the skin but they can't get into it. I've never felt I've ever got real value for money from them. I'm much happier using agencies on specific projects or to achieve specific objectives rather than just having them on a blanket retainer because you think you need to have one. My in-house team is my retainer.

So, as you can see, a holistic approach to a company's communications is the only one that will work.

- Journalists need good stories so don't waste their time giving them stories that are substandard.
- When you give a journalist a good story, you are actually doing them a favour. They have column inches and airtime to fill and anything you can do to help them should be appreciated by them.
- When dealing with agencies, spend time on getting the brief right and ask what value they can add to your present communications efforts.

SIX

Crisis Communications

None of us likes to think the unthinkable, but every business needs to plan ahead to scenarios where crisis management comes into play. It is all too easy for the media to dictate the agenda during a major crisis and it is therefore the task of senior management to try to take control of the situation.

Any one person within an organisation, or the organisation as a whole, can be targeted by special interest groups, or some major disaster can strike without notice. Only by being prepared and anticipating the needs of the media can companies hope to get through what can be a very trying ordeal relatively unscathed.

At Heathrow Airport, for instance, many emergency scenarios are rehearsed regularly. Twice a year an aircraft is deemed to have crashlanded on one of the runways and a complete rehearsal of all the emergency services swings into operation. The airport's press office is fully involved in the rehearsal (usually carried out in the late evening and into the early hours in order to minimise disruption) and the local 'resident' journalists from the national press are invited to do their damnedest in getting a fictitious scoop for their respective papers, including doorstepping airport workers and emergency crews. All participants treat the incident as real and the only thing they know in advance is the date; not the time, venue or details of the incident. By co-operating in this way, both press officers and resident journalists have already built up trust between them and are more likely to co-operate when the unthinkable really does happen.

The most important lessons to be learned during times of crisis are first and foremost to understand the needs of the media and that they have a job to do in meeting deadlines and filling column inches or airtime. To answer 'no comment' to a journalist is the stuff of red rags and bulls. If they have to fill their allotted space this can lead only to speculation on their part and you will have a bigger job to try to kill off rumours that will spread like wildfire.

Stick only to the facts and never make assumptions, as they will be quoted back at you at the most inopportune moment! Journalists will understand if you tell them you need time to check out the facts – and anyway, they would rather paint a true story than one based on supposition (well, most of them would at any rate!). But if you tell a journalist that you will get back to him, ensure you do so in a timely manner, even if it is only to say you need more time. Not knowing what is going on is the one thing calculated to increase speculation.

Although it is not possible to anticipate every possible crisis within a business, there are some things that can be done in advance to minimise the problems at a time of crisis. *De minimus* there should be a contact sheet listing all the telephone numbers and addresses of the executive board, senior management and key individuals out of hours so that they can be contacted at short notice.

Key players need training on media interview techniques since there is nothing worse than a company spokesman looking shifty or answering with long pauses or umms and errs during an interview. (Yorkshire Electricity even goes to the lengths of putting forward for interview wherever possible executives who speak with a Yorkshire accent to add credibility to their being a local business.)

A room that can instantly be turned into a media centre – perhaps even equipped with ISDN line and microphone for live radio interviews – is also a good idea if at all practicable. It should be quiet (in terms of low noise interference) and have a number of telephone lines for any visiting journalists as well as Internet access. They will appreciate having facilities laid on for them that make their life easier, and your business will be less inconvenienced by them in the long term.

An airline crisis is easy to understand and visualise because of the drama associated with it. So let's stay with that industry for a moment and hear from Iain Burns of British Airways, formerly of American Airlines.

When I first went to American Airlines, they had a very good working crisis communications plan. And if you looked at what would happen in Europe – this was a corporate plan written in Texas, remember – the Europe section said, 'Seek advice from your European colleagues.' So it wasn't really that helpful! Effectively we wrote a European plan for them.

Overall it was a well-executed plan, which we sadly had to use on three occasions while I was there. The main aspect of the crisis communications plan was that mentally, once they get over the initial shock and surprise, people want to know what is their role in life with this crisis.

I think you can have the most comprehensive plan but you need a big arrow pointing directly at you saying, 'Your role is x, y and z' (and those x, y and z can be a matter of bullet points). When people see that, they know what their direction is and they can see there is someone directing them in the right way, and so it starts to work right away. That's the most difficult aspect of a crisis plan. When I've worked on plans, I've always tried to find the role of the individual.

At British Airways, we have specific training for individuals. Now clearly you have to plan for a scenario where a crisis is going to happen at 3 a.m. on a Sunday morning rather than at 10 a.m. on a Monday morning with everyone sitting at their desks. As long as you have people trained in a variety of roles and they know what their roles may be, as and when – 24/7, you're away.

Obviously the airlines rehearse quite a lot – in fact in the next nine months we'll be having at least four exercises and I'll have two different guises throughout, but I know what my funda-mental key ones will be in the event of a real crisis. In fact, I had six of my colleagues just this morning working on an emer-gency relief aircraft right down to the detail – and I think a lot of it is down to the detail – working on what's in the emergency bags, rather than just saying, 'Have a manual in your briefcase in the office.' We go way beyond that.

So our communications people will always have two bags permanently packed in here, and updated with cash, clothing and a whole load of other things that would go in there. That's just one aspect of what they need to know – where's my bag, where do I go, who do I report to and so on.

I was fortunate in that we had taken part in a major 48-hour exercise with BAA plc at Heathrow, so our plans with American specifically for European flights had been put into place. When a subsidiary company – American Eagle – had crashed in Indianapolis with 63 fatalities you could argue that it was a small regional flyer serving a major international airline – but in this case one in seven were Brits. So there was a lot of British interest and we were able to put the plan into practice.

American, through legal reasons, has a very clearly defined way of looking after customers and relatives of the survivors, so it's very much a question of the communications pieces linking in with the rest. There was always the confidence that we had the plan in place because you have to realise that any day now it could happen.

Apart from crashes there are other crises we have to plan for. You can have extortion, hijacks and so on, and within each situation you can build in a whole load of other things. Every airline is concerned with when they should release the passenger list. They might be made available on the Internet before the authorities have had time to tell the next of kin. How do you deal with issues like that?

There was an exercise at BA when an aircraft had theoretically crashed in Kazakhstan. There was no radio contact with the local station manager who didn't have a satellite phone. So we couldn't talk with our manager in Kazakhstan. Where do you go from there? Well, obviously you go and buy a load of satellite phones. In this exercise that's where the role-play ended. We had to say, 'Useful lesson learned. Let's get some SatComs.'

Most airlines work their crisis communications in a similar way, and there is a growing belief that IATA [International Air Transport Association] is a good arbiter and a good way of looking at how we can all be uniform in our crisis management. No matter the brand or the name of the airline with which you work or wish to be in communication, we're all in

*the same boat. It's all about restoring public confidence in
flying, so the name of the airline in this case is irrelevant.*

Well, of course, not all crises are as immediately apparent and dramatic as that. Some crises take a long time to develop and are not
always recognised for what they are until almost after the event. Some
companies unwittingly turn a drama into a crisis purely through lack
of communication; others have a crisis plan in place and run it as if
they are on autopilot to great effect.

We have devoted the next section to one story, which amply
illustrates a number of crisis scenarios and the communications
surrounding them.

How Camelot's Numbers Finally Came Up

Dianne Thompson, as CEO of Camelot, has been through several
major crises. If you want to know about crisis communications and its
management – look no further! Dianne is, at the time of writing, also
President of the Chartered Institute of Marketing.

She joined Camelot on 3 February 1997 as their commercial opera-
tions director, long before the company had become 'controversial'.
Most people had never heard of Camelot and simply thought of the
National Lottery as a company in its own right.

Crisis No. 1

But as Dianne Thompson recalls, the first major crisis hit the company
within two weeks of her joining.

> *A national newspaper had acquired a stolen copy of a strategic
> brainstorming session that the board had in January about
> what else Camelot could do to raise money for good causes and
> also to see there was a life beyond the lottery for Camelot, in
> case we ever lost the licence.*
>
> *They ran with the headlines 'Plottery' plastered all over it,
> telling their readers that 'Camelot bosses seek to take our lottery
> overseas' and 'Cloggies will steal our dosh' and all that kind of
> stuff. You could call it typical tabloid stuff.*

Crisis No. 2

In July of that year, Camelot had another crisis to contend with when *Marketing Week* acquired a stolen copy of their draft annual report and published details of the directors' bonuses. The lottery operator had to take *Marketing Week* to court to get the stolen document back.

> Marketing Week *argued that they shouldn't give it back because it was annotated and therefore it would reveal their source and it was an editor's privilege to protect his source; but we argued that it was price-sensitive. Although we're not a listed company, our then-five shareholders were listed. (It could have had an impact on De la Rue and ICL's results because it published not only what the bonuses were, but also what the profits were). And so the judge ruled in our favour. As the document was stolen it had to come back.* Marketing Week *appealed immediately. The document in question was held in a solicitor's safe until we won the appeal.*

Dianne Thompson told us that when they eventually got the document back there was not a single annotation on it.

> *We sent it to a forensic lab in the Midlands. A very detailed report came back showing that although most of the pages were first-generation copies, there were some pages of which many, many copies had been made. Presumably someone had painted out the annotations and then repeatedly photocopied the pages until you couldn't see where the Tippex had been. So we never did get to find out whose copy it had been.*

Fat Cats

As unwelcome as these two crises were, morale at Camelot was also very low because of the so-called 'fat cats' episode. Chris Smith, the Culture Secretary, had publicly attacked directors for awarding themselves large pay rises and bonuses, and the national press saw Camelot as an easy target.

There was the famous photograph of Sir George Russell, our then-chairman, Tim Holley and David Rigg, our director of external relations, walking along Cockspur Street when Chris Smith had summoned them in. That photo got used in the media time after time. It's a very unfortunate shot because it was very windy and ties were blowing all over the place, hair was blown about, none of them had their jackets done up and they all looked rather grim.

Crisis No. 3

In January of the following year – 1998 – Camelot found itself in the throes of the Snowdon-Branson libel case where Sir Richard Branson was accusing Guy Snowdon, the Chairman of GTech, and one of Camelot's shareholder-directors of trying to bribe him into dropping his lottery bid for the first licence.

Within the space of 11 months, three major crises had changed the face of the company. Instead of there being the Lottery with a small company behind it, the public perception had suddenly changed to the Lottery having a group of 'fat-cat' men in grey suits behind it. The demands on the communications strategy and management had changed dramatically.

Original Communication Strategy

Dianne Thompson again:

The strategy that our CEO adopted (and quite a different one from that we adopted when we lost in August 2000) – was that we should 'go below the parapet', not fight back, stay really quiet; and hope that it would die a death. So we didn't chal- lenge. We were caught on the back foot on both occasions – with the instance of the stolen documents because obviously the Q&As had been ready to go out with the annual report about what the bonuses were. (If you had known the facts about the bonuses, most people would have thought that for the risks those people took, they were actually pretty reasonable.)

But, of course, we weren't given the opportunity to explain because the information was out there before we knew it and led to probably one of the worst weeks in my career where, for four days, the media were just running riot and we really couldn't stop it at all.

Then we were very fortunate that the Director-General of the CBI started getting involved behind the scenes. He was saying that, at the end of the day, we were a private company and Government has no right to say what bonuses or not we should earn. The CBI started it off and then the IoD [Institute of Directors] came out in our support as well, and gradually the Secretary of State pulled back and a compromise was reached. This was that those original directors would actually pay an element of their bonus to a charity of their choice.

I think it was unfair that they had to do that. Of course, although the general public doesn't appreciate this, the annual report relates to monies that had been earned in the previous year. So, it wasn't as if they had suddenly been given a lot of cash that they could say, for instance, 'I'll put 10% over there'. Some of them had actually spent it totally. It was a real problem for them.

Camelot decided on a strategy of trying to 'fade into oblivion', and not retaliating on anything, and for the best part of two-and-a-half years it didn't matter what anybody wrote about them, they just didn't retaliate in public, and only demanded corrections if an article was absolutely blatantly untrue and something had been written that would cause overt damage.

Staff Reaction

Camelot's staff hated it.

They thought it was grossly unfair and we got to a stage where our annual MORI survey had as one of the questions, 'How proud are you to work for Camelot?' and we got a score in the high 80s which MORI tells us is unbelievably high. The norm is around 56% and in the top ten the average is 65% and in this we're at 87% – something like that – unbelievable scores.

That result partly comes from the 'Dunkirk spirit' – let's all stick together because all the others are attacking us. However, the question that we never asked, which I think would have been a more interesting question is: 'We know you are proud to work for Camelot; but how proud are you to admit you work for Camelot?' and the answer to that would have been quite, quite different, I think.

Peer Group Perception

Dianne Thompson told us that this came home to her when she attended the *Marketing Week* Annual Awards Dinner as a guest of someone from M&C Saatchi. Her name wasn't on the guest list and nor was her company; she was simply entered as a guest of Bill Muirhead.

They were going through the awards and it was a typical marketing, rowdy, raucous evening – lots of wine, lots of cheering, standing ovations and that sort of thing. Unknown to me we had been nominated for two awards, which immediately tells you we hadn't won, as the organisers didn't know there was anyone from Camelot there so they hadn't arranged for someone to be there in case we won an award.

We got to the first one, which was for the Most Profitable Brand and we were down as the National Lottery, not as Camelot. Marks & Spencer actually won the award category, I think, but we were universally booed. It was just awful and terribly embarrassing for me at the table.

I can't remember the second award – the Most Successful Brand Launch, or something we were up for – and exactly the same thing happened again. There were only three times that whole evening when people booed – twice for the National Lottery and once for the Marketer of the Year who was Rupert Murdoch. (So at least we were in good company!)

I went home and I was really quite upset by this and it changed me overnight, because I thought, 'That's so very unfair' because Camelot is a really good company; and it's just not fair that people – particularly my peer group – should react the way they did. The general public who read the tabloids, that's one thing, but my peer group who should actually realise and who do know that the launch of the National Lottery was so successful, is another. What other brand can say that it has had 94% of the adult population playing on that Saturday in 1996? I mean, what other brand has done that? And even today – seven years on – we still have 29 million players on a regular basis. It's unbelievable what it's achieved. I can't take any credit for it, but it was a fantastic launch.

Relating this achievement to the reactions at the *Marketing Week* Annual Awards Dinner, Dianne Thompson commented,

A marketing group should have known better really, so I was quite angry the next day. That's what changed me. Whereas before, if I got into a taxi and I was going to our office in Cockspur Street, I would say, 'can you drop me at the bottom of Haymarket' rather than say 'Would you take me to the National Lottery office' because I had done that a couple of times and I got a real earful. It would always start off the same way. 'Oh, are you a winner then?' and I would say, 'No, I actually work there', and I'd get, 'Oooh, bloody Fat Cats' and so on. In the end you stop saying it. But not any more – as you'll see!

Time for a Change

Talking to her staff at that time, Dianne Thompson found that people were very proud to work at Camelot, but when they went out to dinner and somebody asked, 'What do you do?' they wouldn't say what they did. In the early days she herself used to say, 'I work in retail' because she had come from a retail background.

These reactions made me determined that one of my key tasks going forward was to change things so that people were not only proud to work for us but were also proud to say that they worked for Camelot.

My predecessor really didn't want to start fighting back until we got into the run-up to the bid [for the second licence] itself.

The bids were submitted on 29 February 2000 and so in the back end of 1999, from about October, we started putting out some rather carefully constructed messages about what we had done. Our bid-winning strategy (which nearly didn't work for us) was that we would try to get external accreditation for a whole variety of things that would prove to the world that we are the best lottery operator in the world.

Camelot had an excellent track record that they could publicise. They were the youngest company ever to get ISO 9001 certification in the UK and only the sixth company to get BS 7799, which is the British Security Standard – and the other five were all clearing banks. They were also the youngest company to get Investors in People and, at that time, Camelot was the only company with all three accreditations.

They also took part in an Ernst & Young survey among the top 30 lotteries – and were ranked first, in terms of technology and security as well as services to players, and services to retailers. So on the back of all these public plaudits, Camelot constructed a communications plan to start putting these messages out to the world at large. Obviously they were also communicating internally through more formal channels. (They have an internal newspaper called *TeamTalk* and an internal glossy magazine called *Camera*. *TeamTalk* is the more serious one where they describe what is happening in the business.)

Identifying Targets

It's always been quite straightforward to identify who our key targets are. We've always been very conscious of who our stakeholder groups are. Obviously we have our shareholders who are very closely involved in the business – in the sense that each shareholder has a representative on the board and we have 10 board meetings a year – so it's not like a perhaps more normal situation where you see the shareholders only at the AGM and a half-year briefing or something.

We also have something called the Communications Group – a public affairs group on which every shareholder has a member, and that is chaired by our director of external affairs. That meets on a monthly basis, so our shareholders are well briefed through that forum as well.

Our other stakeholders include our staff and we were obviously communicating with them through our formal communications. We were in a very peculiar position when we were actually writing the bid because we were put into official 'purdah' with others of our stakeholder groups – such as the distributing bodies – which went on for almost two years. DCMS [Department of Culture, Media and Sport] were only allowed the occasional formal briefing, but we weren't allowed to communicate with the distributing bodies at all, which was a major problem.

Be Prepared

Dianne Thompson feels that there is no doubt that the National Lottery itself suffered as a result of having nearly two years of slow-down because of the protracted bidding process for the second licence. Camelot was quite restricted in terms of whom they could communicate with, especially the distributing bodies. This meant that a lot of joint work, which had been planned to get the good cause stories out to players, had to be out on hold.

We held a press conference on 28 February, the day before all the bids went in, to explain what the key highlights of the bid were. That was quite well received really. On 29 February we actually did our first head-to-head with Sir Richard on the sofas of GMTV (which was the first time I had actually met him). As the press conference the day before had gone pretty well, my then-head of external affairs said, 'We'll do GMTV; we just won't tell the Chairman until afterwards.' In fact, we did pretty well that morning because, sadly for Sir Richard – it must be very difficult in his position: 212 businesses and you can't be an expert at everything, can you? – he had been given a brief that had been slightly misunderstood and got some facts wrong, which gave me the opening I needed to get my messages across.

There was one thing in particular I learned from that. It was to make sure I'm never in a position when I'm taking on head-to-head someone who knows far more about the business than I do because you can so easily get exposed. That's what happened really and we came out of it pretty well. However, we decided on a strategy where we would be low-key from the time when the bids went in, so that was the last day we did any interviews.

A New Communications Strategy

The decision of the successful bidder was to be announced on 1 July, and Camelot decided they wouldn't communicate anything else about the bid before then. They would keep very low-key and only when pressurised would they say anything. Their reasoning was that they didn't want to put the Commission in a difficult position because the less that was made public about both bids, the easier it would be at the end of the day for the Commission to justify its decision. The People's Lottery, on the other hand, appeared to be drip-feeding things out about what was in their bid.

We were just very circumspect really. I have to be honest: we were quietly confident. The mood of the staff here was very confident. We briefed them on only the very short topline headlines about what was in the bid; the things that we had more or less said in the press conference. We really didn't communicate with them very much at all apart from Tim, who was still then CEO, going around saying that we were quietly confident, not complacent, and encouraging people to keep concentrating on the basics. Make sure we don't have any mistakes now, which could cost us the licence. Concentrate on the fundamentals and hopefully we should be home and dry.

Yet Another Crisis

But fate once more took a nasty turn. In the spring of that year a fault was found in the software supplied to Camelot by GTech. If a ticket got jammed in a terminal when the lid was opened (which happens very infrequently) it caused a problem. This was a very unusual fault with a very low incidence of occurrence. The fault had come to light when GTech were doing some routine maintenance on the software and they fixed it there and then.

At the time the CEO of GTech in the UK and the Chairman of GTech in the United States apparently discussed whether they should tell Camelot and whether they should tell the National Lottery Commission. The UK CEO was of the opinion that they should pass on the information but GTech's senior team in Rhode Island thought differently.

I can only guess that the reason they decided that they shouldn't was the fact that the software problem wasn't unique to us in the UK. And therefore by going public with it there would have been problems elsewhere. They were very lucky, and so were we, that the transactions that it had impacted were very few in number – about 140,000 out of 14 billion or something like that. It had only impacted people who had matched four numbers and out of that 140,000, a few people had been short-changed by up to £3, although the vast majority were underpaid by just £1.

In the great scheme of things it wasn't that huge. But nevertheless it brought into question GTech's integrity. That was a bit of a nightmare. We briefed the staff here and Tim sent a note out as to what was going on but there wasn't very much that we could say. We weren't quite sure what the outcome would be

We were working quite hard with the Commission to find a solution as to how we could improve the management of our supplier and to what extent they would be happy for GTech to continue. (We had already taken them out as a shareholder by this time but they were still our major supplier.)

We received a carefully crafted letter dated 29 July 2000 from the Chairman of the National Lottery Commission saying they were now minded not to pursue the issue of GTech not being fit and proper – i.e. they were OK.

We then briefed the staff here that it had been a close call, but we had got through it. GTech were OK, so we were back to where

we had been . . . a great bid, a great track record and we were
quietly confident again. Then 23 August came and of course we
had lost. And we lost in a spectacular way.

The National Lottery Commission announced that neither bid was
acceptable but that they were starting a new process – to negotiate
with one bidder only: the People's Lottery. Apparently the People's
Lottery had two problems with its bid, while Camelot had just one:
GTech. The Commission felt they couldn't trust GTech as a major
supplier.

Eventually, when it was all over and we had won, we did say to
the Commission, 'We were misled by your letter of 29 July saying
that GTech were OK. What was that all about?' The dilemma the
Commission had was that if they had said in July, 'You're out of
the race because GTech's not fit and proper', then how could
they have let us carry on until the end of the first licence? So
what the letter was really saying was that we would be allowed
to limp home until the end of the licence.

It was the Wednesday when we lost and we were absolutely
shocked. I hope there is never another day to match that. We
were all so quietly confident – although I hope we weren't
arrogant; we were certainly not complacent but we worked
very hard on that bid.

Personally I had worked every day on that bid since Sep-
tember, apart from Christmas Day and Boxing Day, until the
bids went in on 29 February – that was a Tuesday morning. The
previous weekend I had actually come in on the Friday morn-
ing and did not go home until 4 p.m. on the Sunday afternoon.
We were all the same – we were across in the warehouse col-
lating the document. It was massive. Everybody was exhausted
but we certainly weren't complacent. We had worked hard.

It was a big shock to lose and on the Thursday we took stock
of what we should do. There was a bit of a mix among the team
whether we should fight or not because the view was we had
written a great bid and we had a great track record, the GTech
problem was supposedly sorted, but we had still lost. We had to

consider that there was a different agenda here. We had to ask, was there somebody saying it was not going to be Camelot or more likely saying we want Branson to have a go? And in that case even if we could get back in the race we would just be wasting our time.

Risk Assessment

Camelot knew that to go to court would have cost them a lot of money if they lost and if it really was all over, the only sensible thing would have been to reduce costs as much as they could – not least because of their fiduciary duties to the shareholders. Their QC, David Pannick, told them that he thought that, at best, they had a 20% chance of winning a judicial review, assuming they were granted one in the first place.

In the UK, some nine out of ten judicial reviews fail and never before had an operator successfully challenged its regulator. The QC's view was that if they did get a judicial review, the judge might give a ruling that what had happened was grossly unfair but actually wasn't unlawful. After all, there's nothing in law that says you have to be fair as long as you are acting within your powers. So he thought the judge would sympathise with Camelot but conclude that there was nothing he could do about it. Dianne Thompson again:

We had a long debate on that Thursday about what we should do. On the Wednesday I had been like everybody else – shocked and tearful. We had all gone down to Yates wine bar in Watford and had had a few lagers or whatever – while the People's Lottery was photographed in Holland Park drinking champagne. But I was angry; it just wasn't fair.

That was the thing that incensed me most really. We Brits believe in two things. One is fair play and the other is queuing! I get incensed about both of those! I had said all along, 'If we had lost in a fair fight, of course we would be gutted but if at the end of the day people with experience could genuinely look at the two bids and actually say this is far better' then I could have accepted that. I would have been gutted because we would have lost our jobs, but I could have accepted that. But what I couldn't accept was that the 800 people here were going to lose their jobs in an unfair way.

Decision Time

It was clear that it had to be me who led the fight. Ironically when Tim in December 1999 first offered me the job to take over as CEO when we won, I didn't actually say 'yes' straightaway. He offered me the job on the last day before the Christmas break and I said I needed to think about it. For my entire career I had worked hard at keeping a low profile and keeping home and work quite separate. I knew this would be a higher profile job than I had ever wanted to do before. Actually, I had no idea how high a profile it would end up being.

I told Tim I needed to talk to my daughter and the people in my family that it would impact upon and I would get back to him after Christmas. I talked about it with my dad and with my daughter and decided that it was my dream job. (I'm not sure in hindsight, knowing all that was to come, whether I would have made that same decision.)

However, on the day after we lost, the discussion went along the lines of, well, if we are going to fight it, it will be very high profile and you're going to have to do it, Di. You're the face of Camelot – although I was only CEO-designate at this point. It was therefore my choice. Was I prepared to do it? I felt so passionately about it that I said, 'yes, I was'.

Time for a Radical Change

That being agreed, we decided that our media strategy should be based on two or three principles. We decided that we should take virtually every opportunity that we had for media inter-views – be it Newsnight, *the* Today *programme and all their* 'horrors' (I could never have previously imagined that I would end up in front of Paxman!). Second, we would review our position on a daily basis and see what the media were saying. We would put a plan together of our key messages throughout that period of fighting back. Third, we would target specific media – we identified specific journalists and we decided who were our friends, who were neutral and those who were absolutely anti-Camelot.

Obviously there were some people who were very pro-Branson and anti-Camelot. So if there was a positive story that we wanted to get out we went to our friends because we knew we would get a sympathetic hearing and accurate reporting. But we tried to limit damage in other areas.

On that Thursday we decided we were going to fight back. On the Friday we announced publicly that we were going to court and we got our court hearing on the Friday afternoon. (The judge was extremely fed up because it was the Friday of a bank-holiday weekend!) We got a call at 3.20 p.m. to say we had to be in the high court at 3.40 p.m. at the latest. Fortunately our office is literally a 10-minute run from the court.

Our main concern at that point was that as the National Lottery Commission now knew that we were fighting back they might try to do a deal with the People's Lottery at the weekend. They might then sign the pre-licence agreement. (As it was a bank-holiday weekend there would have been three days they could have been working on it.) If so, when we got into court the following week it would have been a done deal. We therefore asked the judge for an injunction as well as the right for a judicial review.

He refused to grant us an injunction but he did get the Treasury Solicitor and the National Lottery Commission to agree to have no conversations with the People's Lottery over the weekend. That agreement took that worry away. We were in court again on the following Tuesday and this time a media frenzy was building. We won the right to a judicial review on that day and when we came out of court the media were there *waiting. By this time they were quite excited about what was going on and it was a pretty interesting story.*

We became the underdogs during that period and got sympathetic treatment from virtually all of the media – even from people who had not been particularly pro-Camelot before. By the day we came out of court having won the judicial review, it was like coming out to old friends. Comments like, 'Well done, Di!' and things like that were called out to us. I can understand all too easily how some people allow the attention to go straight to their heads when they are the media's darlings and they can do no wrong.

Camelot's new strategy was to identify what they classified as 'friends', 'middle-of-the-roads' and 'not-friends'. Then, on a daily basis, they reviewed what had happened in the media that morning and anything that they needed to correct. For the first time in their history they challenged everything that was not completely accurate. They asked for letters to be published if the mistakes were serious enough or else they wrote, simply so that a letter was held on file at the offending publication. One of the spin-offs of this new strategy was the effect it had on staff morale.

Internal Communications

The staff here were thrilled to bits that we were fighting, although we tried to manage their expectations that we probably still couldn't win the case even if we won the judicial review. We said they shouldn't think we could necessarily win, but we would go out with a bloody good fight and with our heads held high because we didn't deserve to be treated as badly as this. The staff were really up for that.

But we had a problem. On the day that we actually had lost – 23 August – some of our staff had heard it on the radio or on Ceefax before they heard it from us because we were sworn to secrecy until 12.58 p.m. The press conference was taking place at 1 p.m. and we had everybody who was in the building gathered on this top floor. We tried to get everybody else into our regional offices too, but we weren't allowed to brief before 12.58 p.m. The regional offices had got TV screens on and some of them saw the announcement on the BBC before we were able to tell them ourselves – which was just awful.

Camelot realised that they would need to create a fast and guaranteed effective communications system for internal staff whereby they could get messages out to their people extremely quickly.

Cascading

We created a verbal cascade process working basically with the CEO starting the cascade, giving the briefing to about 15 people who immediately do their own cascades. Some of the people who are cascaded to are then responsible in their turn to phone someone else. Everyone in the organisation has a 'buddy' so that if you're on holiday or off sick your buddy has to make sure that he or she gets to you as a matter of priority. We can get round the whole company – all 900 staff on 13 sites – within 20 minutes. That works incredibly well for us and we still have that system today.

Every Monday morning I have an executive team meeting at the end of which we agree what is to be cascaded today and then each director will go and cascade to their teams. During the fight-back process we held regular verbal cascades even if there was nothing particular to say; that way our people knew that we were being as open and as transparent as possible. That really helped morale here because, as you can imagine, it was a real emotional roller-coaster.

We had great highs like the day we won the judicial review and great lows as well. As well as the cascading process, we also use internal e-mails and shared folders and all that sort of thing. We use the shared folders site so that any message that has to go company-wide is posted there or through the internal e-mail. We also have a staff consultative forum in which every department has an elected representative. ACAS oversee the elections, so it's all very transparent. The forum meets once a month and our HR director sits in the forum although he's not a member.

Open Forum

Whenever possible, I try to go in for the first half-hour and do a 'state of the nation' talk but, if there are issues that we are debating as an executive team, these will be shared at the forum so that the elected representatives can go back to their constituents and consult with them. They then come back to us with feedback about what people think. This is their vehicle. Because, in the main, it is anonymous – just your representative talking on your behalf – they tend to be open and frank.

One of the things I was most proud of was when we had Gerald Kaufman and the Select Committee here after we had lost, but before we won the case; and they had asked to meet some of the staff. Some of the staff consultative forum came into the boardroom for coffee. We hadn't briefed them beforehand. We'd simply said, 'Be open and honest and do your best to answer any questions. Don't be intimidated.' Gerald Kaufman said, 'Are you unionised?' and a chap from our security team put his hand up and said, 'No, we're not unionised; but we don't need a union here because we have the staff consultative forum. We have an active and open dialogue with the management that works incredibly well.' It was absolutely brilliant!

We also have TeamTalk. It looks slightly dull because there are no coloured pictures in it, but it's very factual and in there is a column on the staff consultative forum so everyone can know what the forum is talking about and people can write in with their questions. So I think our internal communications have worked extremely well.

Battle Scars

Dianne Thompson recalls only too well how, when Sir Richard Branson finally conceded defeat on 10 January 2001, Camelot were in a pretty poor shape because, not only had they lost the six months that the delay took (between the decision date in August and 10 January) but they had also lost momentum.

Although they had decided to fight the original decision from 23 August, there was still a strong likelihood that they would lose their appeal. So because of their fiduciary duties to their shareholders, the decision was made to start closing down anything in the business that was not part of the original licence conditions. This included all the development and market research on new and interactive games, which now had to be scrapped. All in all, the whole process cost them some 18 months in development and momentum.

When we had actually won we had been up high but very soon after we were very low. One thing I didn't anticipate was how many staff we would lose and in fact our attrition in 2001 was 31%. You can't blame people leaving when they have mortgages to pay. It looked like it was all over and although the staff were delighted we were fighting, if you have mouths to feed you have got to get a secure job. Sadly, and very reluctantly, a lot of staff left but I didn't anticipate that it would be that many.

Now again we're 900-strong with 325 of those having joined us in the past nine months. Last year was a nightmare in many ways. We didn't have the public traumas that we'd had the year before in the period of fighting back but, actually, we had the business to run while being short of a third of the staff.

It's not the kind of business where you can say, 'Sorry, we can't do the draw on Saturday because we don't have enough people to do it.' Life has to go on. In addition, the two-thirds of staff left not only had to run the business, but they also had to go through the whole recruitment and induction process to get the new third in. On top of that we had to replace all the terminals – there was the threat of a £5m fine per day for every thousand terminals we were short from the start of the new licence. That rather focused the mind!

Tuesday 11 September [when Al-Qaeda attacked the World

*Trade Center] hit us like many other people because the ter-
minals were coming in from the USA and, at one stage, I had
2000 terminals sitting on the quayside at Boston and couldn't
get them out. I had components coming from Korea into New
York and couldn't land those because there were no planes – so
there were all sorts of traumas.*

*What we did last year, which I think was a very brave move on
our part, was to change our culture. When we look back where
we were in February, we were a Company that was battle-
scarred and weary; we were also totally risk-averse because
we had been saying to people, 'Don't get anything wrong. Any
major mistake now could cost us the licence.' So we had
disempowered people. Nobody was taking decisions at all –
except the senior executives – in case they took the wrong
decision. We didn't have any creativity or innovation because
we could not begin anything new. We were the proverbial
rabbits in the headlights – frozen.*

*In a sense, we had gone through one crisis in terms of losing
and then winning again, and then we had yet another crisis in
terms of recreating the company with a third of the staff missing
– although the third of new people coming in weren't battle-
scarred and weary. They came with new ideas and fresh
enthusiasm.*

*There's no doubt that the Lottery was damaged by what went
on during that whole period. If you had said to me at the time,
'There are two ways of winning the licence – the easy way or the
hard way' – I would have said, 'I'll take the easy way'. But
actually, having won through the fight, I have seen some real
benefit from that too because, for the first time, Camelot has a
human face. People have now seen us as normal and fairly
nice people with no airs and graces, no pretensions, and so our
image has started to improve with the general public, although
very slowly.*

Lessons Learned

Dianne Thompson admits that, as far as crisis communications are concerned, many lessons have been learned during her time with Camelot.

I have a press cuttings service which sends me daily press cuttings at home delivered at 7 a.m. every morning so I don't actually step out – as I did just once to be doorstepped about something that I didn't know was in the papers. Because the press cuttings service are cutting from midnight, any major story breaking that we don't know about gets fed straight through to Sue Slipman who is our director of external affairs and she will phone me.

We operate a 24-hour newsroom service and Camelot are now renowned in the media for never having a no-comment policy. We always will give a statement of some sort on whatever it is. We never hide anything; we will always be open and honest.

Only the newsroom (around 16 people) and I are allowed to speak to the press, so if a call comes in from any member of the press the rules are that it has to get referred down to the newsroom straightaway. They will then take the call but not necessarily respond immediately to the question. Depending on what the question is we might say to them, 'We'll get somebody to ring you back.'

With all that crisis experience, my advice is always to be as open and as honest as you can. Although this means you will sometimes get some flack, it's better that way than to say, 'No comment' and let the media put whatever spin on it they want. Sometimes that's easier said than done, and sometimes it can hurt personally. But it goes with the territory.

Many communications professionals would agree whole-heartedly with Dianne Thompson. When faced with a potential crisis, think through what your objectives are, plan carefully your messages and consider all your audiences, don't run away from unpalatable situations, and be seen to be open, fair and honest.

Coping with a Crisis – or a Scandal

As we've already seen, regardless of their size, most firms will sooner or later find themselves having to face the problems associated with a major – and possibly very public – crisis that at the very least can badly affect morale among the company staff, and in the worst-case scenario can lead to the closure of the business.

Crises come about for a number of reasons, but invariably things can be made better or worse by the level, content and timing of your corporate communications during this episode in the company's life. A company's reputation is crucial to its future success, and at times of crisis you simply cannot afford to let the media have a field day with negative articles knocking your company.

In all these things, professional advice is worth getting since specialists in PR and general publicity have a good understanding of how the media work, and they know the kind of things that editors are on the lookout for – as well as the moves that will surely be to your detriment. Regardless of your coterie of business contacts and per-ceived standing in the business community, when there is a crisis it really is a time to call in the professionals.

At times of crisis one of the golden rules is not to trust anybody – even (or especially) those within your company. Just when you want to speak to people about it all you must keep your own counsel. This may sound unduly harsh, yet it's often those nearest to you who, with all the best intentions in the world, can neatly 'drop you in it' because they haven't thought out the consequences of what they are saying.

It's also absolutely crucial that those within your company should be comprehensively briefed on everything that you are making public and putting out in carefully crafted and rehearsed statements so that they don't undermine those very statements by ill-thought-out com-ment.

One of the biggest problems for companies is to decide on the level of reaction to bad publicity. If you under-react by keeping silent, gossip can get out of hand because of the 'no-smoke-without-fire' syndrome. We've all seen it many times in the press. On the other hand, over-reacting can be just as bad. Many situations can be made worse by trying to crack a peanut with a sledgehammer. Because many people are too close to the problem to be able to take a step back and take an overall perspective, this is the time when talking to someone who is not too closely involved is essential if you are to get a thoroughly objective view.

The golden rule, however, is found in the old adage that honesty is the best policy. Even little white lies can come back to haunt you at a later date, and if you are seen as untrustworthy – even if what you have said is strictly true but leaves out some important facts – you will be judged as having misled your public and you will be branded as an unreliable person or company.

Finally, they always say that the graveyards are stuffed full of 'indispensable' people. (Many a fallen politician has learned this the hard way.) Arrogance, conceit and being seen to be aloof are your worst enemies and whatever else you do during a crisis, make sure you are seen as a 'man (or woman!) of the people'. How else do you think the likes of Sir Richard Branson can do no wrong in the eyes of the general public?

In short, here is a list of general action points for any company that finds itself in a crisis:

1. Don't go it alone. Get professional advice straight away. PR agencies know the media better than anyone else – and you'll have enough on your plate.
2. Don't be arrogant. Just because you're a big fish in your own industry or company pond doesn't mean that you can rely on your self-assuredness and conceit. Pride comes before a fall.
3. Remember the people who have got knives out for you? Were you nasty to them? Anyone you were nasty to even years ago could think it's your turn. Be nice and bite your tongue.
4. Do watch your back. What happened in ancient Rome when Caesar got stabbed is still the most likely scenario today. Trust nobody.
5. Be most diligent in briefing people. Both inside and outside your company, properly thought-out statements, which are then used to

brief well, will ensure that 'helpful friends' cannot undermine you unwittingly.

6. Be honest – *really* honest – wherever you can. Lies have a horrid habit of coming back to cause trouble later.
7. Don't under-react. Under-reacting generates gossip.
8. Don't over-react. Cool reality will ensure that you don't over-respond.

SEVEN

Means of
Communication

For messages to be understood and accepted, they need to be imparted in the most apposite way appropriate to their content. As you can see from Figure 7.1, there are numerous methods of communication, some of which are by their very nature better than others. Each have their advantages and downsides and the sensitivity of the specific message needs to be brought to bear on the decision as to which is most appropriate. You also have to decide whether certain information should be 'pushed' at people or whether they should 'pull' it from a knowledge bank. Considerable resentment of technology-driven 'pushed' information was found, which led to a backlash in 1997 and most people would prefer to 'pull' the information when they want it. Depending on what the information is and how crucial and time-critical it is, the decision is yours.

Ways and Means

Face to Face

By their very nature, face-to-face meetings are two-way communication processes – even if one were to involve only a manager letting off a string of invective at a subordinate. (The subordinate would, after all, be displaying a number of unconscious messages through their body language at the very least.) The most basic form of communication is between two people in a head-to-head meeting. Information flow there is two-way and it probably has the most potential for checking comprehension on both sides.

Figure 7.1   *Ways and means of communication*

Not only do the words convey meaning, but also body language helps in conveying the right signals to the other party, showing that what they are trying to put across is being picked up by their audience. Sensitive issues can be tackled, which might not be possible in a less personal forum, and here the instant feedback one gets can prove crucial.

In terms of company resource, however, such meetings can use up an inordinate amount of time. For appraisal, recruitment or counselling, their use is unequalled, but the success of such meetings is always dependent on someone taking the lead and the planning and thought they have put into it.

There can be major problems with such meetings, however. Just because one party doesn't say much doesn't necessarily mean that they are in agreement with what is being said. And specifically if there is no immediate record made of the meeting, it is surprising how often the different parties leave with a totally different view of what has been agreed. It is notable how many sets of minutes are disputed, even if they are received within a couple of days. And you can guarantee if you leave sight of the last month's minutes until a week before the next meeting, there will be huge disputes in content and accuracy. Some public bodies are notorious in 'doctoring' minutes so that they reflect what policy should have dictated was said, rather than what was actually said and noted!

For a one-to-one meeting to be successful, the following 'rules' are essential:

- If the meeting is to be formal, an agreed time should be set and a venue found that will ensure no interruptions.
- Objectives should be set and time allocated for the different topics to be covered.
- Topics for discussion and relevant documentation should be understood by both parties prior to the meeting so that any 'homework' or preparation can be done before the start of the meeting.
- The meeting should be as participative for both parties as possible, allowing enough time for both sides to state their views.
- At the end of the meeting, agreement should be reached on actions to be taken by both parties and, if appropriate, a written summary of what was agreed should be made available to the other participant.

And as Andrew West of West Associates points out:

Feedback is the most important thing any human being can get. We can't function without it. It's absolutely critical. If we don't get it, we invent it and that's the danger. For instance if there is a possibility of redundancies, but we don't know who, we try to fill the gap and assume it's us – we assume the worst as a general rule.

Formal Meetings

Formal meetings are, in many ways, an extension of the head-to-head meetings outlined above. They can be great in moving a team forward together in the fastest practical way; but they can also waste an incredible amount of time with participants wondering why they even turned up in the first place.

In Saudi Arabia, one of the biggest food manufacturers brought in consultants to help them make their business more efficient and to use their resources more frugally. Competition was intense across the

Middle East and the company wanted to break into new markets outside the kingdom.

Whether language proved a problem, or there was a cultural breakdown is not clear. But orders came from the chairman that in future, in order to make more efficient use of time throughout the company, all managerial meetings would last an agreed length of time, which was not to be varied under any circumstances. At the start of the meeting it would be agreed by the participants how much time was to be allocated to each topic and one of the participants was nominated to be the timekeeper. Five minutes, then three minutes and then one minute before the end of each allocated period, the timekeeper would warn the meeting that time was running out, and if discussion had not finished by the end of that allocated period, it was cut short and the meeting moved on to the next topic.

Somewhat unsurprisingly, many meetings ended with little agreement on anything having been reached, with the result that many people felt they were wasting their time even turning up. Even less surprisingly, the company lost its eminent position within its marketplace, and its hopes of expanding at that time across the Middle East came to nothing.

For a formal meeting to be successful, preparation is all-important and the end result should be clear actions and responsibilities so that all feel that the situation or project has been moved forward by everyone's participation.

- Objectives should be set so that everyone knows what it is that is trying to be achieved.
- Dates and venues should be set as far in advance as possible in order to give everyone the opportunity of attending.
- An agenda should routinely be circulated before the meeting together with any background reading so that participants can be up to speed before the start.
- Conclusions on each topic should be summarised with action points agreed before moving on to the next topic.
- Minutes of the meeting should be circulated within 24 hours so that all actions expected of the participants catch no one unawares.

Cascade

As we saw from the Camelot story, the ability to cascade information quickly is essential for staff morale as well as continuity of message. There is sometimes a tendency to over-complicate the cascade layers and means but, for an effective cascade of urgent information, telephone is the preferred means.

In organisations where not everyone has immediate access to the Internet, or the habit of logging on, the use of an e-mail cascade can leave crucial people out of the information loop and thereby put the company in jeopardy. It is better to identify the urgency of the message before selecting the means.

Take the IT director of a multinational, for example:

We have a cascade process. Any key information will be announced at the operations board meeting, which we have once a month, and then the area directors will pass that on to the group managers who will take that information out to the branches.

This process isn't perfect because we sometimes find that something communicated at the operations board meeting doesn't necessarily find its way down even as far as the group managers. In essence we really would be better off with a flatter communications structure.

The problem is that there is no directive: 'You will say this.' So what tends to happen internally is that there is a perceived elite who tend to keep this information because of the old adage, 'Knowledge is power.' I think it's a natural thing that people want to guard useful information that might just give them the edge over their rivals. And when we have such an entrepreneurial ethos within the company and everyone is trying to outdo the other one, then they are unwilling to co-operate as groups.

There are times, however, when information cannot be held back and must be communicated to everyone in the company with the minimum of delay. Following the 11 September attack on the Twin Towers,

British Airways – along with the entire airline industry – was concerned for the public perception of flying generally as a viable means of transport, especially as people stayed away in droves and cancelled flights in the immediate aftermath. Iain Burns of British Airways:

> *The management briefings were weekly, so you'd get the chief executive talking to the top management every week and these messages were always cascaded. Then after the first few weeks had passed it would become a debate round this table whether we should wait for two weeks but we thought, 'No'. We reckoned we should keep it weekly because the minute you go fortnightly, 'Crisis over, guys! Let the good times roll!' That can be the biggest communications challenge.*
>
> *How do I say to members of British Airways, 'Look, it's not over' because what do they see now? They see the planes are full, and if we go back to a monthly management briefing they're going to see 1988 all over again and they'll think we're going to be making nearly £1bn profit. Oh, no, we're not! So we have to keep explaining to the staff – albeit that they're an educated bunch out there – and they can see the movements in the share price because we have an awful lot of staff who hold stock in the airline.*

Team Briefing

A natural precursor of the concept of cascading information is that of team briefing. This became all the vogue in the 1980s when managerial structures started slimming down and the top-to-bottom path started to shorten. The idea is that information starts at board level and cascades down through a network of managers, supervisors and team leaders to reach the entire workforce; the reverse is – in theory – also meant to happen, with ideas from the shop floor cascading upwards through the dizzy levels of the managerial heavyside layer to reach the boardroom.

Theory is not always translated into practice. Most of us have at one time or another played the classic game of Chinese whispers where a phrase such as 'sardines and peas' transmogrifies into 'more beans and fleas', or something equally as absurd. This is a prime example of how communications can go badly wrong, as we identified in our section in Chapter 3 on 'Causes of Ineffective Communication'. Nevertheless, it's a timely reminder that such a simple and natural thing as committing a succinctly worded missive to a chain of people to pass on verbally is fraught with danger. The problem with a message being passed on up or down the line is that invariably the teller's own prejudices or agenda colour the transmission with the result that there are subtle differences between the original message and the final one received.

However, used effectively, team briefings can provide the rudiments of a communications system to disseminate information. With the ready availability of electronic communications methods though, there are often better means of achieving this.

For team briefings to have any chance of success:

- Objectives and content need to be clearly defined.
- A briefing pack will often help reinforce the core messages.
- Local information and messages can be added to the core material by the local managers.
- Any action points from each meeting should be minuted and agreed.
- A feedback system for any unanswered questions should be incorporated into the system so attendees are not left with unanswered questions.
- Senior and middle management should fully 'buy-in' to the system, otherwise the lower ranks will feel that it is purely a top-down process with no reverse information flow.

We're including here a typical set of team briefing guidelines as an aide mémoire.

A Typical Set of Team Briefing Guidelines

The Six Basic Principles

1. *Face to face*: Allows you to check understanding and take direct feedback. Meetings must be open and allow two-way communication.

2. *Small teams*: Groups of between four and 12 people encourage participation. Ideally teams should have a commonality of purpose so that whatever is communicated is relevant to all.

3. *Workgroup leader*: The person who briefs the team should be the line manager responsible for the results of the team.

4. *Regularity*: Monthly briefings are ideal, but whatever the frequency, briefings should be held regularly. A regular slot (e.g. first Wednesday of every month at 2 p.m.) is preferable as everyone then knows where they stand. Try to publish the dates (on notice boards, intranet, etc.) as far in advance as possible.

5. *Relevance*: As people are more interested in what actually concerns them, the core brief should be only a starting point. Two-thirds of what is briefed should relate to the group's immediate concerns.

6. *Monitoring*: You need to monitor what is briefed, how regular meetings are, and whether the meetings are successful.

What to Brief

1. *Core brief*: Do not read the core brief verbatim. It should be put in your own words and where necessary additional explanation or comments should be allowed for. All company material should be briefed positively since you are part of the management team.

2. *Local information*: This should be department-specific, including operational information, customer perceptions of the department and so on. This information should be provided to workgroup leaders by departmental heads when their direct reports are briefed.

3. *Workgroup information*: The information for this section is supplied by the workgroup leader who will review specific tasks and last month's performance.

4. *Performance measures*: All work groups should have performance measures that relate directly to their tasks. The workgroup should be given a measure of their own performance and, where appropriate, how the company as a whole is performing.

How to Brief

1. *Prepare*: Note down what you want to cover and have your per-

formance figures ready. You will not be effective if you try to busk your way through the meeting. Be sure of what you are going to say, particularly if there is a difficult topic you want to discuss.

2. *Be positive*: Any outward sign of lack of enthusiasm will inevitably rub off onto the rest of the team; in which case why bother with the meeting at all?

3. *Record action points*: Use a flip-chart or some other highly visible display and get feedback immediately, rather than wait for someone to ask questions at the next meeting.

4. *Further meetings*: If an item crops up that requires lengthier discussion, it is often better to suggest a further meeting devoted to that particular topic.

5. *Record the meeting*: Although some managers require full minutes to be kept, all questions and action points should be recorded as a minimum so that they can be acted upon and progressed.

Suggested Agenda

1. Welcome all to the meeting and note any absentees for later briefing.
2. Start the meeting with good news or a success story as this will have a positive effect on those assembled.
3. Give the core brief.
4. Give details affecting the workgroup including:

   - Follow up from last meeting
   - Last month's output
   - The coming month's workload
   - Performance measures
   - Discussion of any problems
   - Discussions of areas for improvement
   - Recognition of individuals who have done a good job
   - Group discipline issues (but never individual discipline issues)
   - Future initiatives.

5. Give other information, such as on health and safety matters.
6. End on a positive note.

7. Brief date and venue for next meeting.
8. Thank everyone for attending.

Walking the Talk

A well-known utility company (which is best kept anonymous here) had a severe problem with staff morale. 'How come our employees appear to resent the directors so much?' wailed one of this misunderstood group to his chief of communications one day. 'They always appear resentful, never offer anything constructive in a meeting and appear sometimes even to go out of their way to avoid us.'

Questioned as to how often he went out of his way to meet his own staff, he admitted that if he wanted to talk to any of them he summoned them to his office where the business could be conducted efficiently and the employee could then return to his desk in the open-plan office just across the corridor outside. Asked if he knew where anyone sat in the open-plan area, or to name some of the junior members of staff just yards away from his office door, he had to admit he didn't know many. He called in the favoured few on his phone and they came when he called them.

It seems amazing to think that anyone can be so blinkered in their treatment of fellow people within the company, and this might well be an extreme case in point; but it is surprising to us how often when we go into companies as consultants that some of the so-called senior personnel appear to behave in such a cavalier manner.

'Walking the talk' is a popular buzz-phrase that came over from America and basically describes the process whereby senior management go out of their way to walk around the workplace, talking to people at their own desks or work stations and gauging the atmosphere by what on the surface can appear as small talk. Carried out successfully it builds an element of trust and breaks down barriers so that everyone feels part of a team, rather than as one of a them-and-us situation.

Walking the talk works best when:

- The interpersonal skills of the manager are well honed;
- Employees at all levels are approached, rather than just key individuals within the team;

- Reinforcement and positive comments are made, rather than finding an excuse purely to criticise;
- Preparation of key messages is done as well as 'homework' on individual staff members so that they feel the manager takes an interest in their personal welfare;
- Time is given to the staff members to let them have their say; and
- The manager is seen as being approachable and ready to listen, rather than using the meetings as an opportunity to get his point of view across

West Associates' MD, Andrew West, gave us a practical example:

I know a general manager in South Africa who had breakfast meetings with the whole factory once a month. There was no way that he could know everything that was going on or answer everyone's questions but he was there, he was having breakfast with them and he was listening. I think that, in a basic sense, that is all that people ask: that the top guy is there and that I have a chance to pose a question. So it's showing willing and being available that is as important as the message being put across. This is the unstated message – I am available, approachable and willing to listen.

There is another general manager I knew who said, 'I'm going to spend a day working in each area of the business – including a day in the factory' – and it was written up in the staff magazine showing this man assembling things on the assembly line doing the job that the ordinary guys were doing, only rather worse! That kind of gesture makes a tremendous impression.

Social Time

Hopefully, long gone are the days when senior management go to lunch in a different works restaurant or canteen from the majority of staff. There are exceptions, of course; how many companies still decide to send their directors first-class to a conference or trade fair and expect the rest of the team to travel second-class? What messages do the senior management believe this sends to their workforce?

Meeting people in 'dead time' such as in lunch breaks or group travel time can deliver huge benefits in terms of mutual trust and understanding. Tim Melville-Ross, a former Director General of the Institute of Directors, calls this process 'breaking bread' with someone. By talking over a meal, a relaxed atmosphere usually ensues and allows the two parties to get a better mutual understanding of the issues up for discussion.

For such socialising to work well, it is important to:

- Know what it is that you want to talk about;
- Not pressurise anyone to attend but to invite people to meet only if they want to;
- Make it clear to those who are not invited that the people you are meeting are representative of the audience you wish to talk to and that their exclusion in no ways is a reflection on them; and
- Arrange the logistics in advance rather than relying on ad hoc arrangements at the last minute.

Events

Depending on who the audience is that you wish to reach, there are various types of events that can act as a conduit for 'pushing' information out, as well as for 'pulling' in feedback and other useful information.

Conferences and Trade Shows

'Going public' and exhibiting your goods or services at a trade show or participating in a conference can be an extremely good way of letting the world know about your company's offerings. There are numerous trade events held up and down the country that can be guaranteed to get your target market attending and thereby being in a position to receive the messages you are trying to communicate.

Apart from the main business of the conference or trade fair, a great deal can be achieved in the way of forging relationships and alliances in the bars, lobbies and restaurants. Here, the 'breaking bread' principle we outlined above comes to the fore and people can exchange ideas in an informal and relaxed atmosphere: classic networking in the most valuable sense because it is based on a group having a common theme or objective at the time.

Organising conferences and exhibitions is a costly business and takes a great deal of planning to make them worthwhile. There is nothing worse than a trade show that is a flop since you are then effectively laundering your dirty washing in public at such events. Costs have a nasty habit of spiralling out of control unless very tight financial management is imposed. There are many examples of such events being seen as a waste of time since no one sat down to determine the objectives before starting on the costly exercise in the first place. Without objectives, how can you possibly determine whether you have been effective or not?

In planning a successful conference or trade show you will need to:

- Agree on the objectives well before you start on the logistics;
- Decide on your target audience;
- Carefully plan the content and length of each item;
- Choose a suitable venue;
- Rehearse all your participants so that each knows why they are there and for what they are personally responsible.

Speeches and Presentations

As a means of conveying information, speeches – and, to a lesser extent, presentations – are not very efficient. But where they come into their own is in the impact of conveying emotion and a 'wow!' factor.

A number of speech agencies around the country – such as Select Speakers, Speakers' Corner and Speakers UK – can find suitable professional speakers for almost every type of occasion; often just to give the keynote boost at the start or end of an event to fire delegates up about what is coming next or what has preceded them.

If effective graphics or choreographed events, or some other gizmo to attract attention are used, a powerful sales message can be imparted, which will linger in the brains of the recipients long after the event is over.

One favourite trick of event organisers, for instance, is to let off a thunderflash just as a new product is unveiled to an expectant audience. The effect is dramatic and gets the audience buzzing. But beware the pitfalls! One computer company we know of was showing off its new product range to its sales team in a local hotel. Unfortunately no one had thought to tell the hotel management about what they intended to do. If they had, maybe someone would have thought to switch off the automatic fire sprinkler system and saved everyone (and the equipment) a good soaking!

One of the many problems associated with giving speeches or presentations is that, frankly, some people are just not up to the task. We have all, at one stage or another, sat through a dire presentation given by someone who is embarrassingly awful and who, one suspects, just wants the floor to open up and swallow them whole! They may be boring, or long-winded; they certainly fail to capture their audience's attention, and will often by their very presence ruin whatever effect was hoped for in the long planning stages.

Often, this will have resulted from nothing more than stage fright on the part of the presenter. We regularly come across board members and 'captains of industry' who are prone to become gibbering wrecks when standing up in front of an audience. Coaching can help, but if they show no signs of improvement it is often kinder to let someone else stand in and perform in their place. Chief executives take note!

Some speakers, conversely, don't even bother to research their audiences, ignore their brief and totally fail to ask themselves what the audience is expecting or wanting to hear. Either that, or they leave their preparation so late that the end result can sound rushed or lacking in 'flow'. Many presenters put together their speeches the night before their performance, which is why the general standard is often so low.

By definition, speeches and presentations are best at 'pushing' information out to an audience, since audience participation is necessarily limited. Remember, too, that the audience will remember only a few key messages. There's a parallel to that famous piece of research in the 1980s when a number of people were asked at around 10 a.m. to name the three top stories on the previous night's TV news bulletin. The majority could come up with only one, in addition to an 'off-the-peg' story. So much for retention!

For a successful presentation, Carol Jones of Select Speakers believes the following points must all be addressed before putting on an event, or it may be less successful than it should be or even prove an expensive folly:

- Agree what the objectives are for the event before even starting to prepare a speech.
- Ask yourself whether slides, PowerPoint presentations or handouts will help or hinder the message you are trying to convey. If they will, prepare them in plenty of time for your stage crew to be able to prepare them from their point of view.
- Rehearse, rehearse, rehearse . . . until you have the pace and delivery right, and fit the time slot allocated.
- If you can record or videotape your presentation rehearsal, you will find that you are your very own worst critic!
- Identify who exactly your audience are (are they existing clients, target clients, invited guests only, the general public, local/national media . . .?).
- Why are the audience there? (to be informed, persuaded to buy, to have a good lunch, meet colleagues in the industry . . .?).
- What is/are the reasons for holding this event?
- What do you wish to achieve by holding this event?
- Is it a serious event or do you wish to include an element of humour?
- Is it a 'hard sell' event?
- What budget has been allocated to this event?
- Who (or which department) is funding the event?
- How important is it that the event is a success?
- For whom in your company is it important that the event is a success?
- Whose job (or status) is 'on the line' if the event fails?

- What will make this event especially attractive to your guests?
- Do you need a 'big name' to attract people to come?
- Remember that a company chairman, chief executive, sports personality or celebrity may not necessarily be a good speaker or even enjoy speaking.
- Similarly, just because someone well-known says they speak at events does not, in itself, make them interesting as a speaker or the right choice for your event!

Roadshows

Roadshows are a very good way of reaching huge numbers of people across a wide geographical spread. In some ways they can be seen as an extension of the previous type of event, repeated over and over again at each venue.

When, in the mid-1990s, Yorkshire Electricity wanted to break the bad news that 5500 of its people were to be made redundant, it was decided to hold a number of roadshows around its home territory, which in those days (before deregulation had set in) stretched from the Pennines over to the Humberside coast. Five venues were chosen and at each show, a minimum of three board directors would be present. Speeches would be given on the present financial circumstances that the company was in, the new threat that deregulation was bringing in and the effect that redundancies on such a large scale would have.

Despite some initial opposition, the decision was made to break with tradition and allow members of the audience to ask questions *that had not been submitted in advance*. Not only that, but if one of the directors did not know the answer to a question he was asked, he would undertake to give a written reply in the next edition of the staff journal. So as to kill any rumours of the directors giving answers tuned to each particular audience, a full write-up of one of the roadshows would appear in the staff journal.

Perhaps none of this appears particularly earthshattering, although at the time this was considered high risk. But the results well justified the course of action. A widespread distrust of the company directors (which in some ways had been exacerbated by the reluctance for anyone to face the workforce without pre-prepared statements) was considerably lessened and allegations of manipulation of one depot against another all but disappeared overnight. In short, trust began to be re-established despite the news that redundancies were on the way.

Of course, roadshows can be used for broadcasting good news to the troops and themed events can considerably spice up what could otherwise be boring or mundane. Probably the most useful benefit, though, is the personal contact that can be achieved between the senior management and their people or, if performing to an external audience, between a company and its clients.

When planning a roadshow:

- Allow at least three months for the planning and implementation. (You might be surprised how many little things seem to take up so much time.)
- Make sure you undertake a cost-benefit analysis before committing your company to such a project, as roadshows notoriously eat up your budget.
- Plan in a 'wow!' factor to get people to talk about the event long after it is over!

Telecommunications

Ever since Thomas Edison gave his much-fabled demonstration of his newfangled telephone device to the Mayor of New York, telecommunications has played an ever-increasing role in every company. It's almost impossible to imagine corporate life without the telephone and all its peripheral devices, and hardly a month goes by without new equipment and possibilities opening up.

Even without the ubiquitous presence of the Internet, telecommunications has come of age. It is now routine for callers to bypass switchboards and secretaries, and call centres have become a way of life for many companies 'doing' CRM (customer relationship management), but the downside is that many companies fail to encourage their people to answer one another's phones when there is no one at that desk.

By their very nature, phones rely on two-way communication, but they have a number of disadvantages, which many people simply do not appreciate.

- Although it might be a good time for *you* to make the call, your recipient might well be busy with other things. Effectively you are assuming that your agenda is more important than theirs.
- Calls rely on both sides taking notes to have any kind of record of the conversation.
- Since there is no eye contact, it is easy for one party to assume the other party has fully grasped the meaning of what is being said and will not overlook some of the minutiae of the conversation.
- Because many people do not prepare their calls in advance, they can be unstructured and the conversation can wander off at tangents to the main point of the call.

Voice mail, which has largely replaced answerphone machines in many companies, has its own problems, too. For instance, many people find great difficulty in coping with a one-to-no one situation when they are expecting to speak to someone at the other end of the line. Because they have psyched themselves up for some type of interaction, they feel confused and unprepared when having to have a one-sided conversation. In many cases they will not even have thought about the possibility of having to ask someone to call them back because the time that they called was convenient to them; they now have to be prepared for the fact that when the other party calls back the time may not be convenient to them.

One of the most important things about telephone usage, however, is the impression it creates when someone rings up from outside to speak to someone inside your company. How often have you telephoned an organisation to find the person on the other end of the line has an offhand manner, doesn't seem to know the answer to your question (or even where to direct your call for a proper answer) or even puts you through to the wrong department?

It never fails to amaze us how often, when we go in to companies to conduct a communications audit for them, that temporary staff and untrained staff are put on the switchboard to deal with incoming calls. How can it make any sense for a company to offer as the very first point of contact with the outside world a person who is so unsuitable for the task in hand? What kind of impression do they make?

Telephone Conference Calls

Most telephone exchanges now offer audio-conferencing facilities to link up three or more people simultaneously. At its most simple, a split telephone line linked to two handsets can be used for two people in the same office to talk to a third party.

There are also specialist 'black boxes' available, which plug into a telephone socket and act as a wide-area microphone and loudspeaker combined. This makes it possible for many people to be sitting in a room and talking to a third party elsewhere.

If the telephone conference is between three or more separated parties, care must be taken that the quality in each area is good enough for all conversations to be easily heard by all participants. If one of the parties is overseas, there may well be a time lag between outgoing and incoming signals because of the delays introduced by satellite communications, and this can be a problem if people are not used to waiting an unnatural length of time between the end of what they say and the start of the overseas contributor's speaking.

When setting up a telephone conference it is a good idea to:

- Agree a meeting time well in advance;
- Distribute any documentation via e-mail or fax before the start of the conference;
- Agree on a conference chairman who will call the other participants and take responsibility for cuing in each participant to the conversation; and
- Explain to people who are new to this medium the etiquette needed whereby you need to identify yourself whenever you speak since confusion can otherwise easily result.

Fax

Do you remember, in the early days of fax machines when companies routinely used telex to send written communication across the wires, the Luddites who predicted that fax machines would never catch on? But of course, like most networks, they did catch on once they had got beyond a critical mass of users.

Nowadays the fax is essential in any business, and no longer do we have to rely on thermal paper, which fades after a short period of time, and machines that jam up with infuriating regularity. Newer fax machines are now integrated with phones and answerphones, and many fax programs are available for running on office computers.

With the advent of networked computers, many companies are beginning to realise the advantages to be gained by allowing people to send and retrieve faxes from their own personal computer, rather than having to go and collect them from a centralised fax machine or waiting to have them delivered in the internal mail, which obviates one of the advantages a fax can offer – immediacy.

Plain paper faxes have also made a tremendous improvement in the quality of received items. And because the finished copy can look almost as good as a mailed letter, faxes are not only more immediate than relying on the vagaries of the postal service, but often work out cheaper as well.

Older fax machines are often, however, more trouble than they are worth. Poor image handling – especially for those that rely on large shaded areas – together with curled-up fax roll paper can produce an end result that creates a bad impression and is difficult to read. Jammed fax machines are common and with most organisations rarely maintaining their fax machines, what is sent out is often covered in dirt patches and even all but illegible. The organisation is only made aware of this when a client rings up to complain. After all, they cannot see what the end result looks like.

And given the many possibilities for faxed messages to get lost somewhere between the receiving machine and the person for whom the message is intended, it is surprising how few people ring up to confirm that the fax has been received. At the very least it puts your recipients on notice that they should be expecting your communication in a very short while.

Some other common errors that we regularly find in various companies are:

- Faxes getting lost in the internal post. Sometimes the curly paper has a habit of getting trapped behind a post tray or finds its way into other areas it shouldn't go. (A plain paper fax machine will sort out this problem.)
- Failing to check the fax header when setting up the machine. Not only does your fax number need to be checked, but also any other information that header contains. One company we know was subcontracting out some of its work to another supplier. The problem was that this other supplier was then faxing directly to the clients who could see at a glance that the communications were not coming in from the company they had originally contracted.
- Not buying the right machine in the first place. Many fax machines come with all sorts of extras that are rarely used by the end-user and instead end up confusing them. And how many companies even bother to train their people in how to use the machine in the first place? One of the commonest errors is placing the work in the machine upside down so that the recipient receives totally blank pages (apart from the header of course!).

Audio- and Videotaped Presentations

Sending out recorded messages – either in pure audio, or as a videotape – used to be commonplace a couple of decades back as companies found how easy it was to produce reasonably good quality tapes for sending out to customers or sales staff who were based outside the office.

Nowadays with the advent of the Internet and better multimedia offerings, the taped presentation has languished in popularity. And because people are used to being bombarded with professionally produced communications via their television screens, anything that falls below a critical standard is doomed to failure.

Audiotapes are useful if your audience spends a great deal of time in their cars; salesmen, for instance, can listen to the tapes as they commute to their next destination. But most people have great difficulty writing for the spoken word rather than for the written word, and audio presentations can sound extremely boring or patronising as a result.

Videos can fail for similar reasons. Because people expect to watch broadcast-standard programmes, the disappointment factor is likely to be great if they are anything less than professionally produced. They are also extremely expensive to produce when measured against cost-per-view as they normally involve so many people in the production – scriptwriters, cameramen, sound men, editors, and so on.

Nevertheless, there are plenty of good production houses around, which specialise in producing corporate videos. For your video to be successful, ensure that they:

- Produce a full script outline;
- Agree budgets – these can easily run away if not properly kept in check;
- Produce, and get approval for, a full script; and
- Create an 'off-line' edit to give a rough version of the programme for approval prior to going to the more expensive on-line editing.

Closed Circuit TV

An extension of videotape programming is to run fully-fledged internal TV programmes transmitted across a company's premises or even via a closed user group satellite distribution. Normally this would be appropriate only for large organisations such as multinationals since it is anything but a cheap option; although when normal programmes are not being transmitted, the network can be used for showing teletext messages, which are cheap and easy to produce.

One of the biggest pitfalls in going for this type of communication medium is that to save costs, it is all too common for programmes to fall into the mould of long, staged interviews or talking heads, which rarely work well unless the participants are trained to appear on television, and then only if they have a natural televisual flair.

With the proliferation of telecomms companies offering satellite upload and download facilities, then as a way of reaching large numbers of people in disparate locations it can be cost effective to produce a one-off programme and transmit it via satellite. You can even use satellite technology to stage a live broadcast with interactivity from other remote locations. For product launches, merger announcements or as an alternative to corporate roadshows this works very well and because of its relative novelty value it can easily impress.

However, in negative territory once again, the cost may well outweigh the benefits of immediacy, and if anything goes wrong technically, the entire event can be a dismal failure.

Print

There is such a plethora of printed material about that in order to get a message across to the desired target audience, considerable sensitivity has to be applied to the decision of what printed media to use and why. The comfort zone of printed material for many people still gives a better route for information acceptance and absorption than does e-mail and the screen.

House Magazines/Newspapers

For most larger organisations, the publication of an in-house magazine or newspaper brings a sense of community to the workforce. There is continual debate as to whether a magazine or newspaper format is more appropriate, and there are really no hard-and-fast rules. More important is the variety of content, which can include company news, personal items, departmental run-downs, competitions and social events.

For instance, the BBC's in-house magazine, *Ariel*, contains pages of job advertisements and secondment opportunities together with profiles, news items about the corporation itself, personal adverts, a letters page, general backgrounders and picture stories. The publishers take pride in the fact that *Ariel* is not seen as a management mouthpiece. In fact there have been many occasions when the magazine has reflected staff anxiety over job conditions, for instance, in favour of giving over too much space to the official management line. Obviously this means that the editor has to tread a fine line on occasions, but the magazine has had a loyal following for very many years.

Ariel is actually produced by dedicated BBC staff, but for many companies it would not be cost-effective to have such professionals working in-house. Often it is cheaper and there is more flexibility to contract a specialist firm that produces magazines for many companies. This also gives an opportunity for some of the production costs to be met from the inclusion of advertisements since specialist magazine producers usually have a team dedicated to selling advertising in their papers.

Newsletters

If you are concerned with reaching only small target groups, a newsletter format can be highly appropriate, especially since anyone with a PC can produce a simple format newsletter with one of numerous DTP programs that are readily available.

By their very nature, newsletters can:

- Be produced quickly and relatively cheaply;
- Target specific audiences; and
- Focus on factual information, removing much of the dross found in a magazine-style format publication.

But they can look amateurish if:

- Not laid out well;
- Relying too heavily on clip art;
- The graphical or photographic content is not optimised correctly for the printer involved;
- Deadlines for each issue are not met; and
- The editorial style is poor.

In any company, a newsletter is often high on the list of priorities for communicating with staff. This is true even in the smaller enterprise, although in micro-firms the content and frequency may well have to be structured differently. In a larger firm – anything over, say, 1000 employees – it may well be worthwhile considering moving up to a full-scale newspaper since the individual units making up a large business tend to think of themselves as their own mini-companies and mini-communities.

Good newsletters work. There can be no doubt about that. But they only work if there is enough time and effort put in to them, and a proper budget allocated to pay for them. Not that they need be expensive in the slightest; but know what they are likely to cost both in terms of money and especially in staff time *before* committing to the project.

As we've said before, think what you would want to read about if you were one of the regular staff members picking up the paper, and set it up accordingly. In this increasingly insecure jobs market, you will want to know what could affect the position of your job; you will certainly want to learn how well your company is doing in the market-place and how well it is perceived by others; you may well be interested in new products being planned and you will certainly want to catch up on news of your fellow workers.

The important thing to remember is that the production of the newsletter should be regular – people like to know when to expect it and although it could appear weekly, fortnightly, monthly or even quarterly, the monthly newsletter appears to be the most popular.

Although everyone ideally should be able – and want – to contribute, there should be one person who has overall responsibility. It may be someone wearing a human resources hat, or a local area manager. It could be someone who fancies himself as a frustrated journalist. It could even be your PA. Whoever does take on the mantle of responsibility will certainly expect to co-opt colleagues from other departments to help collect the news – to be the eyes and ears around the company. Ideally each section of the firm should have a representative to feed in relevant news – be that marketing news or notice of a forthcoming inter-company football match.

And it should aim to appeal to everyone. That means that it should aim to cover as broad a spectrum as possible about what is going on around the patch. It's not a bad idea to include a short article written by the section leader or, if you have a small company, it may well be appropriate for you to add in something yourself each time. It doesn't have to be – indeed it shouldn't be – a lecture to your people. But obviously it is an ideal opportunity to let them know what is happening in broadbrush terms about, say, future orders or the general health of the company. Don't forget to include words of praise where praise is due. Generosity of spirit costs nothing but is much appreciated – and remembered!

There are, of course, all manner of things you could put into the newsletter and there is no magic formula about what does and doesn't get in. Don't include things just because they have been submitted, but do remember that people like to read about themselves and about their friends and colleagues. So births, marriages and deaths, who's retiring, who's been appointed, competition results and sporting occasions are all worthy of inclusion. For if there is no light stuff, your people will not find they have the time to wade through heavy diatribes and exhortations for the good of the company.

It would be nice to think that each of your newshounds will be able to write their own little contribution and pass it on to the editor for collation, but life is never that easy! In practice, your editor will find he has to write much of it himself, but if you think about it, that's not necessarily such an onerous task. If the newsletter is only two sides of A4 paper it doesn't take much time to knock the copy into shape.

Even four sides of A4 isn't too much of an imposition for one person to collate, but if you decide to go for this size, make sure you stick to it. Having two sides one month and four sides another sends out the wrong signals – almost that someone couldn't be bothered to get the normal size newsletter out. Remember also that the name and phone number of the editor should be clearly visible, along with a request for future raw news. It's surprising how bashful some people can be when it comes to offering up the kind of material about which they know they would dearly love to read!

If your appointed editor has never done this kind of thing before, you could suggest to him that a good discipline is to have a fixed publication day every month. A raw material box should be the first repository for all incoming material. On, say, the twelfth of each month he should ring round or e-mail all his contacts to cajole or encourage them into sending in late copy. On the fifteenth, he can then start compiling the material for inputting to the newsletter. He may well run off the copies on the nineteenth and distribute to all employees on the twentieth. It's quite a good idea to avoid month ends for this since it's a truism that so much else seems to time itself naturally around then (not least, the month-end accounts!).

It's a good idea to use colour effectively. Not a lot. You don't need a great deal to catch the eye. But a splash of colour in the masthead is worth considering, and one of the easiest ways of doing this is to pre-print your header design using two colours. Failing that, you could use coloured paper on which to print your final offering. But steer clear of boring old plain white! It's an instant recipe for your editor's work of art to be consigned to the I'll-read-it-later-if-I-have-time heap that inveigles its way onto most people's desks at some time or another.

Obviously your editor will want to ensure that his newsletter is distributed as quickly as possible. There's nothing so unappealing, after all, as old news. Perhaps your internal mail system is the most effective way of getting a copy to each member of your staff. Or instead your people could pick up their copies from various collection points around the building.

So you've got it written, it's been printed and it has landed on people's desks. But has it succeeded in its aims? Well, you could always ask for feedback. Correction: you *should* ask for feedback. After all, how else do you know what your people *really* want to read about and whether the current offering hits the target?

A sure indication of whether it is all worthwhile may well reveal itself on the day that, for whatever reason, the newsletter misses its deadline and nothing appears on the expected date. If there is a clamour to know where it is and when it is likely to appear then that's a very good indication that it is valued. If, instead, there is a deafening hush then perhaps it is time to review progress to date!

The Great Debate

As an easy, cost-effective and direct means of communicating with your employees there is little to beat the company newsletter. Or is that really true? Andrew West is not convinced.

> *My own view is that staff magazines in general are not very successful. They absorb a lot of time and money. A lot of people have to work out what to say and then you need specialists designing them – it's a whole industry in itself. Personally I think that written communication is the worst of all types of communications in terms of motivating people.*

On the other hand, Roger White at PricewaterhouseCoopers takes a diametrically opposing view.

> *I have to say I think there is always a place for a good solid piece of paper and I'm pleased to say that I won the argument because after a year or so without one we've relaunched a staff magazine, which comes out on a monthly basis – like the old two used to. A lot of the content you could probably say is the same as that on the intranet, but what you can't do with electronic communications is give that sense of belonging, of seeing faces you recognise, of getting a sense of the feel of the place.*
>
> *Electronic communications is great for pieces of hard information, but it's not very good for creating the personal touch and a sense of belonging. A number of people also tell me that they like taking it home. They can share it with their family, they can read it on the train, and so on . . . there are all sorts of things you can do with paper communication. It's not that expensive to do, it's not that time-consuming to prepare and there's plenty of research over the years that says that people like seeing pictures of themselves. If they can't see a picture of themselves, they like seeing a picture of someone they know.*
>
> *They don't want it to be a mouthpiece for management, so we try and focus on things that are important to the firm and the firm's strategy. But there's much more about getting over a feel of the place, which is a phrase we use a lot inside the firm.*

*We are a very diverse organisation and it's important to make
people feel they belong and have a sense of what that means.*

Whichever side you decide to take, we'll sit firmly on the fence on the
basis that there are valid arguments on both sides! What you've got to
remember most of all is that you and the rest of your workforce must
have good relationships.

Brochures and Reports

When communicating with external audiences such as shareholders,
suppliers and distributors, a good impression needs to be given that is
unlikely to be fulfilled by a newsletter.

Many companies pay a lot of money for the production of highly
polished brochures and company reports, which have a high impact
on their readership, can convey a great deal of complex information
by the inclusion of detailed illustrations and graphs, and are robust
enough to get stored on a shelf for future reference.

Annual reports are a prime example of a means of communication
where a company wants to make a good impression on its shareholders and to pass on the unspoken message that 'We're doing all
right; your money's safe invested in us'.

Almost always produced professionally, company brochures can
turn into mini-books with a wealth of information about the company
that people can dip into at their leisure.

The Right Mix

Because every organisation has so many different audiences with
which it needs to communicate, a fine mix of brochures, newsletters,
magazines, reports and fliers needs to be produced.

Consider, for example, the amount of print that almost all the major
European airports are likely to produce:

- Annual reports for their shareholders (even if the shareholders
  are the local municipalities, such as at Manchester Airport, since
  the managing company still needs to keep the local councils
  sweet).

- Quarterly or annual handbooks for visitors containing fascinating facts about aircraft that land there, lengths of runways, catering facilities and so on (and not forgetting to include some of the key messages that the airport operator wishes to impart to its customers).
- Flight timetables – not just for passengers to check their flight times but, perhaps more importantly, to convey the unspoken message that theirs is a popular destination and therefore, first, passengers should always consider flying from there if at all possible and, second, airlines should consider setting up new routes to these airports, rather than flying to competing destinations.
- Business magazines, aimed at the business traveller and selling the on-airport facilities designed specifically for this very important sector of the market.
- Duty-free magazines, full of tempting offers for the airports' captive audience of potential shoppers, who have nothing better to do for the two hours after they have checked in. (It's not for nothing that airports such as Gatwick have been described as a massive hyper-market complex with a few aircraft parked in the background!)
- Staff newspapers – aimed not just at the airport's own staff, but at those working for the airlines, caterers, retailers, transport operators and others who work in the vicinity. Airports, after all, play a major part in any local economy in which they are based, and getting everyone who works within the complex to buy into the core messages of an airport's operator is an important PR objective.
- Briefing packs, manuals and guides for just about everyone who works within the airport's boundaries; full of rules, regulations, suggestions and, of course, hidden core messages from the operator.

Noticeboards – Get them Read!

One of the most efficient, most cost-effective and most underrated communication vehicles is undoubtedly the company noticeboard. Isn't it ironic that some directors will be happy to cough up lots of money tweaking a publication so that it is *just right,* while ignoring something that is visible by all, is instantly recognisable and, if it is 'serviced' correctly, widely read?

There's no great mystique about noticeboards but, as with all good communications, a little time spent planning what goes on them and how well they are looked after really will make all the difference between success and failure.

Just about every company has a noticeboard, but how often do your people read it? Come to that, how often do you read it? The chances are that if it appeals to you it should also appeal to your fellow workers. Unless . . .

Unless the news is old; unless the board is dingy; unless there's no rhyme or reason as to what is put on it; unless there's no imagination as to the layout of the information; unless it's seen as a propaganda outlet; unless . . . unless . . .

Of course, your noticeboards are different, aren't they? You have already appointed someone with specific responsibility for their upkeep, haven't you? You have explained that their duty is not just to pin notices to it, but to keep it smart and readable. You have explained that they need to check it regularly and to remove the out-of-date material since a noticeboard that gains a reputation for being out of date will soon get a reputation for not being worth the bother of wasting one's time.

But you have also fathomed that there's a lot more to it than that, of course. To catch the eye of the passers-by, noticeboards have to be both visually appealing and, more importantly, they should lead the eye straight to the message being promoted. That means, for instance, having the board divided up into specific areas, so that operational information is not positioned slap-bang against general company information, which itself is separated from personal information.

And often enough, it's the personal information that will attract people in the first place. A notice reminding people to keep the fire door closed is more likely to be read if it is situated near an announcement of a staff social evening. So allow room for personal messages, but do insist that all notices are submitted via the keeper of the boards. That way there is no excuse for one piece of paper partially covering another, especially when drawing pins are in short supply and someone wanting to advertise his old banger of a car to his colleagues will not simply re-use one of the pins that is holding up another notice. (Have you noticed how bits of paper that start off with a pin in each corner somehow have a habit of ending up curled at the edges and being attached to the board by one pin in the top centre? Uncanny, isn't it? – Or is it, more likely, a sign that that particular affiche has been there too long?)

Another thing you might care to ask yourself is whether your noticeboards are themselves positioned in the most effective areas. After all, although you want them to be readily accessible, they shouldn't be responsible for blocking passageways when the contents are so exciting that all your fellow workers will want to read them at the same time. Consider also whether they all have the same look and feel as one another. There's no reason why one noticeboard should have different information from another unless, of course, it is department-specific.

Finally, and perhaps most importantly of all, get your noticeboards noticed! That's not meant to be as daft as it sounds. When, for instance, was the last time you actually *noticed* the state of the carpet in reception? You walk over it so often that it has become too familiar – and we all know what familiarity breeds.

In the same way your noticeboards need to shout out to all passers-by: 'Hey there! *I'm* here! I've got something that will interest *you*!' So be ruthless. Make sure that nothing stays up after 10 days. And ensure that messages are displayed with their sell-by date. That way you will be communicating the fact to all who read them that it's always worth-while coming back for more. Who knows, after all, what gem of information your people might miss unless *they* make the effort to find it out!

With all these different ways and means of communication there are no hard and fast rules. However, there are some fundamental considerations that will mean the difference between your communications being effective or creating a large boredom factor. These are:

- When posting any information on a noticeboard or bulletin board, make sure it is up-to-date and fresh.

- Consider the wording very carefully because other people's perception of what you mean may be totally different from yours.
- Have someone different from the author read through everything to ensure quality and clarity checks prior to releasing information of any sort.
- The most effective communications are where people are with other people – relationships make or break the effectiveness of communications.
- The more arm's length you are from the people with whom you are communicating, the more likely is a misunderstanding.

EIGHT

Electronic
Communication

It's amazing to think of the impact of electronic mail within the corporate environment in so short a lifetime. Literally billions of e-mails wend their way across the world in a blink of an eyelid and the instant communication this offers is truly tremendous.

E-mail

The problems of assimilation of e-mail into a good position into one's daily routine, as well as taking into account the pitfalls of such an instant communications method, are why we are devoting one whole section of this book to the medium. It is both an easy and an uneasy medium, and is often taken lightly when it should be taken as seriously as a hard-copy letter with all the embossed letterheads that might add visual and sensual weight.

In terms of cost-effectiveness, e-mails can outshine many of the old traditional methods of communicating. Think of going through the motions of writing a letter. You have to:

- Compose the words
- Lay it out properly on the paper
- Proofread it
- Print it out
- Address the envelope
- 'Stuff' the envelope
- Stick on a stamp
- Place it in the out-tray or postbox
- Wait for it to be collected

- Wait for it to be delivered, probably the following day
- Wait for an answer – if you are lucky two days after you sent your missive.

Now compare that with e-mail.

- Compose the words
- Fill in the address line
- Proofread it
- Press the 'send' key
- Wait for a very short time for it to be delivered, perhaps on the other side of the world
- Quite possibly get an answer back almost by return.

The biggest danger posed by the use of e-mails is down to the very thing that makes it such an effective medium – its immediacy. People are far more inclined to dash off missives that have been poorly thought out, almost as if they are spoken in a face-to-face meeting without proper thought having been given to the consequences of saying something. E-mails may *appear* to be 'here today, gone tomorrow', but in reality they leave behind a full audit trail, which can so easily cause a great deal of embarrassment at a later time.

Take the now-famous case of Western Provident vs Norwich Union in which the latter had to pay £450 000 after it was shown that scurrilous e-mails regarding Western Provident had been circulating internally within Norwich Union's headquarters. Western Provident were able to get a court order demanding access to Norwich Union's internal e-mail distribution system to prove the rumours that had been 'doing the rounds'.

The problem is that because of its immediacy, it is all too easy to fire off an e-mail when one is excited or angry, and to hit the 'send' button before time has been given for proper consideration. Once you've sent the e-mail, you cannot normally do the e-equivalent of rushing to the mailroom to withdraw your letter. You have to live with the consequences.

Jo Moore at the beleaguered Department of Transport learned that lesson the hard way when she suggested in an e-mail that bad news be leaked out immediately in the aftermath of the 11 September 2001 terrorist attacks. It makes one wonder why she ever decided to put out such a sensitive suggestion in an e-mail rather than just going to talk to the press staff. The incident shows either that she had extremely poor judgement or that she simply didn't understand the medium she was using.

One of the other main problems with e-mail is that it easily undermines personal communication. Many are the examples we have come across of managers firing off e-mailed missives to their staff when they are only sitting a few yards away from them. Yet face-to-face communication is always better than using e-mail, and taken to extremes it can have some potentially damaging effects on personal relationships.

However, used wisely, the advantages of using e-mail to get in touch with colleagues, customers, suppliers and anyone else at a remote location are paramount.

Bulletin Boards

Bulletin boards are now seen as an extremely valuable way of gaining feedback from customers and staff. With the advent of Internet technologies, many companies host bulletin boards for their staff, their customers and their suppliers, and when they form part of a company's intranet they provide a good way of getting informal feedback on anything the company is engaged in.

Roger White at PricewaterhouseCoopers points out, however, that bulletin boards – or discussion boards – have their uses, but are not a universal panacea for internal communications.

> *We encourage people to send in questions – whether it's internal or external – but we're not that convinced about the value of discussion boards to the business, although within specialist areas we do have specialist groups; and within the marketing communications community we are just developing one.*
>
> *Part of the focus is on changing the way people are trained and developed – their standing in the firm – and part of that is*

to ensure that they can talk to one another as part of a community. So we're much more focused on communities that have some sort of common ground – for instance, audit trainees who may want to gossip about the latest exam papers or whatever. What we try not to do is to have a blanket board where everyone can go and talk about anything, because we're not really convinced it's that productive.

Since the advent of the Internet in the middle of the 1990s, communications within companies have changed dramatically. That's not to say that the basic tenets of communicating are not the same, but the different channels and the speed of interaction have opened up a whole new dimension. This speed of transmission has created huge opportunities, but even greater threats and an understanding of the medium is essential to getting the best out of it.

Intranets and Extranets

With all these different means of communication available it is easy to get into the habit of using one over the other – whether or not it is suitable for the message or recipients. Roger White again:

We use a combination of electronic and paper. There is a very good e-mail system and an intranet called 'Knowledge Curve' and everyone has access to that. Everybody has dial-in access so you can get in wherever you like. Clearly there are sometimes issues about speed of access, depending on where you are, but basically once you are into the system you can pick up anything there. We can tell how many people are accessing the intranet and we also do regular research.

Apart from just posting stuff onto the intranet, we also have a regular electronic news vehicle – an e-mailed bulletin – which goes out every Thursday night to tell everybody what's going on. And that has a whole range of issues including the red-hot latest news right through to 'The IT system in so-and-such a place is closing down on Friday night'. There's a mix of things you need to know as well as stuff you might like to read. That has an incredibly high readership. Well into 90% of our people regularly access it.

My internal comms team compile all of that. Together with what goes on the intranet, it is very much seen as a communications issue and not an IT issue. As long as they have provided the basic network for it to work, the rest is an editorial issue. It's an interesting challenge with the amount of people we have working off-site.

We went down the electronic route very heavily when Price Waterhouse merged with Coopers & Lybrand to make PWC. Pre-merger, we had two very good house magazines. But at the time of merger it was seen that we should be at the cutting edge and therefore we should be electronic.

We got a different perspective from a growing international company that has an inadequate communications department, with the result that communications is, at the moment, largely driven by the IT division who told us:

We send a monthly update to everyone by e-mail. We are also rolling out ADSL [asynchronous digital subscriber line] to all our sites, which will allow them all to get onto the intranet too. Our aim then is to use that as a vehicle to communicate with all of the sites.

The intranet was there initially to share information that we needed in head office. But we see its presence as ideal for use for internal communications as well. What we have is 50 sites in the UK and others all over Europe. The CEO can't hope to meet these people all the time so if he were to put his messages out on the intranet, it could well prove to be an invaluable aid in pulling the company together a bit more. The interesting thing is that he can go into a branch now and people don't know who he is because we have quite a high turnover of staff and so they don't recognise him. If we had a picture of him on the front page of the intranet, welcoming them to the site along with his message of the month, it might help.

Another on-going debate is who should have access. Origin-
ally it was envisaged that only branch managers should have
access. But we're trying to say that we can control both access
and security, so that information that is only relevant to one
section can be kept within that area only. However, it must be
said that there is a general mistrust of the intranet because
despite our assurances some people are worried that even
secure information will be accessible by everyone.

To encourage use of the intranet we sent out a weekly
newsletter with: 'Did you know you could find this information
on the intranet . . .?', 'If you go to this section look what
marketing have done . . .' and, for instance, we'll have a
marketing toolkit whereby if you want a standard template for
a letter it will be on the intranet. So really, we've sold the
intranet a lot on the basis of standardisation, giving them
control and making it easy for them. And what's more, it's
accessible from anywhere; that's the main thing.

For any kind of company operating from multiple locations or branches,
an intranet can prove to be invaluable, especially as costs plummet
relatively speaking as usage increases.

Once you have got your internal staff on board, it may well betime
to consider including external audiences as part of your user base.
Among the group's business dependencies, the relationships between
your partners, strategic alliances and customers can be greatly
strengthened by using an extranet. When transferring information,
the implementation of an extranet will enable companies to use the
speed of Internet technologies to reinforce and develop better
relationships, while saving time and money.

The role of an extranet in a business lies somewhere between the
Internet and an intranet with security and protection provided by
passwords together with the usual firewalls. The Internet allows
unlimited access because it is a public forum; whereas an intranet is
purely an internal forum and, as such, allows strictly limited access. An
extranet, on the other hand, allows selected business partners and
customers into the inner sanctum so that only companies who have

the equivalent of a 'most-favoured-nation' status can have access to your company's internal systems. Obviously setting up an extranet has to be carried out both carefully and properly to work for all the partners and customers involved.

It is generally known that the normal business drivers for using an extranet are:

- customer care
- supplier relations
- network management
- sales opportunity
- cost reduction

Within many industries now, extranets are used to provide information, keep in touch with suppliers and distributors, collect payment and improve the whole process of ordering. Through such a site, suppliers can collect payments, information and documents.

In all, business security is paramount, and the mere thought of letting other people into your inner sanctum of core systems makes this more pressing; and so when looking at bespoke or boxed extranets there is a lot of planning before taking one's first step along the implementation path.

NINE

Communication Audits

So where does one start when trying to improve one's communications – internally and externally? Usually, the first thing that is necessary is to assess what your company currently does in this field. The best way to do this is to carry out an audit of what communications you currently use. This is because, if you don't know what the current situation is, you're going to have to make some guesses or assumptions, which could prove to be an expensive waste of time in the longer term.

The purpose of the audit is to find out which communication channels already work, where people would prefer to get their information from, who is credible, what awareness there is generally as to the usage of the different communication channels, and so on. There is also one very important function of a communications audit; it will allow you to set a benchmark against which future audits or surveys and their resultant decisions can be measured.

Audits can come in many forms, but they usually boil down to a survey and/or a compilation of what currently exists. Often, for greatest potential benefit to the business, they are best carried out by an outside firm since, in our experience at least, many people feel perfectly happy talking to complete strangers about things they would never dream of saying in front of their colleagues or supervisors – or even their peers.

Behaviour patterns within an organisation, similarly to within any grouping of people, are fairly quickly established and quite difficult to change. It is only when something new happens within a hierarchy or product range that people tend to break out of their behavioural moulds. This shows itself in the information that is freely given to new people introduced to the company.

In fact, many people we have spoken to in our audits have been extremely indiscreet – though we make a point of reassuring them, and explaining to the board for whom we write the report, that all comments will be unattributable to the persons we interview in order to get the best feedback.

Surveys are conducted on each firm's communications activities and its impacts on the business, including:

- media, customer, supplier and political perceptions
- internal communications
- methodology measured against achievements, staff assessments and departmental restructuring
- writing job descriptions, staff training, motivation and standard procedure manuals

Interviews are then conducted with board directors, non-executive directors, advisers, line managers and communications staff (including marketing, public relations, human resources, design and advertising, and other personnel whose function could impact directly or indirectly on the communications effort).

A specific focus is made on both internal and external communications, looking at the resources deployed and the effectiveness of the efforts, and determining strengths and weaknesses that may not currently be apparent. All the findings are analysed objectively prior to preparation of recommendations, which are made for future strategy and implementation.

There follows below extracts from communications audits carried out by Topspin™ Group for small plcs, which for obvious reasons must remain anonymous. Some of the audit report findings have, of necessity, been left out because they were so pertinent and personal to the companies concerned that they might have been able to be identified. However, the intention is to give a good flavour of the type of thing that can be thrown up in such an audit.

Areas covered would normally include:

- A detailed examination of the various methods of internal and external communications;

- The resources deployed;
- The effectiveness of their effort; and
- Strengths and weaknesses of the company's communications that may not be currently apparent.

Methodology

Throughout the communications audit a series of interviews is normally carried out with directors, line managers and others who may have an impact or input into the communications procedure – formalised or not – utilising a variety of attitudinal and motivational techniques to delve behind surface perceptions.

Individual interviews can be sought through a series of pre-coded questionnaires designed to ellicit tactical information, ensuring that consistency of the core information is recorded and that there is no collusion by the interviewees.

Examination is also made of written and electronic methods of communication, together with library, research and presentational materials.

Internal Communications

Within the audit there should be a study and analysis of the various methods of internal communication, including lines of reporting, internal briefing papers, team briefing/cascade information, information gathering and material clearance procedures, together with any internal printed material.

External Communications

An audit should be made of the messages being given out externally to a variety of audiences, to establish whether they are being received correctly by the recipient or misunderstood. A clearly defined set of corporate goals and market positioning must, of course, already be in place for this to be feasible.

Corporate Literature, Advertising and Sales Promotion

An examination should be made of all currently existing and proposed literature, brochures and other forms of communication, both for design and written content, to provide a holistic and constructive view as to whether it meets key defined criteria and the purposes for which it is intended. This will include any advertising and sales promotion carried out by the company, whether it be overt product and service advertising or whether it is 'sideline' advertising in the form of directory entries, recruitment advertising or above the line in national or regional publications, special offers, sponsorships and competitions.

Complete Information Cascade

Consideration of the way information is cascaded from staff to customers and other external audiences – such as the media – should be given and should include the means of the cascade.

IT Audit

Although this is primarily a communications audit, the way the messages are delivered is of prime importance and therefore no communications audit can be complete without an in-depth look at the technologies employed.

This is often best undertaken by an outside firm who can bring an objective view. From the information gleaned within the audit, analysis, presentation of the options for improvement, planning, approval and implementation can then be undertaken with the full weight of the board behind it.

Extracts from Communications Audits

What follows is a series of extracts from communications audits carried out by Topspin™ Group on behalf of a number of clients.

Although many of the recommendations are company-specific, you will see that much may be pertinent to companies generally.

We begin with:

Summary, Positioning Paper and Urgent Actions

There are a number of opportunities and serious threats that will affect the strategy and the subsequent business plan for the whole of the group. These need to be addressed urgently as they strike at the very heart of the way companies will perform in the future. Because of the speed of change in the use of Internet technologies, the focus on customer relationship management systems, and the resultant take-up within business of the communications opportunities offered, time is of the essence in considering, implementing and launching a revised strategic plan for the group.

Board Meeting

The proposals contained in this report have been prepared confidentially for the board and we believe they have the potential to cause a quantum shift in the group's position, market share, public perception and perceived value.

The change in distribution channels brought about by new technologies affects the balance of everything. Two of the group's subsidiaries in particular, which trade in information, could face annihilation in the next few years if the threats are not addressed and opportunities are not taken.

The group needs to rethink and perhaps place itself at the apex of Internet and broadcast technologies to take advantage of the new climate in which combined content and distribution companies are a force to be reckoned with.

Websites

The existing group websites need urgent review if the group is to be taken seriously. Websites should be constructed with a view to easing communications with all audiences and to building up massive and comprehensive databases of potential prospects and customer information – all properly qualified and therefore of great commercial value to the group.

Branding

All branding implications need to be reviewed, including web domain names and trade marks with their branding implications, which need to be reviewed urgently. We will discuss this and the implications of it in our next meeting because of the dependencies and negative impact of the current situation.

E-mail

A comprehensive e-mail policy across the group needs to be agreed and implemented without delay. There are considerable anomalies and inconsistencies between different subsidiaries and between different departments.

The use of e-mail signatures must also be implemented to comply with the Companies Act and to take advantage of the promotional and other communications aspects available.

Intranet – Knowledge Management and Internal Communications

The board should consider the setting up of an intranet/extranet with a phased implementation plan in order to enhance pooled knowledge management and internal communications. The lack of an intranet is hampering speed of production as well as causing communications lapses and misunderstandings because of the time taken to make any information available throughout the group.

The chief executive and senior management should be able to access accounts, sales figures, etc. as well as private e-mails and conference facilities when travelling.

A series of thought-through plans needs to be devised to enable the cascading of information. For instance, it is essential that all people within the organisation can be contacted by telephone in an emergency with information within 30 minutes of the board deciding that they should be told. In this way no one will be unknowing of a crisis or the group's position on it and be caught out – as before.

The demand for access to the Group's central information systems from remote working will increase as the activities of the Group diversify and globalise. Good foundations, in the form of a well-thought-out but easily operated intranet/extranet will prove its worth within months. (Most well-planned corporate intranets pay for themselves within three to six months of inception.)

Investor and City

Provision should be made for automating the system of supplying information to investors and analysts. In addition, adequate background information on the group and its up-to-date activities should be available on the website so as to be a source to which telephone enquiries should be directed.

IT Skills

An urgent review of IT and skills sets needs to be carried out within the whole group.

Extranet

Suppliers and partners need to be given passworded access to the group's extranet in order to improve information and cash flow.

Subsidiaries

A network based on a hub is urgent in most subsidiaries, as is Internet access and e-mail for all – particularly in the line of business that is the group's core activity.

Within the artwork subsidiary this is particularly urgent, as is Internet access and e-mail for all. This should be bought in and implemented with a view to the hardware being able to withstand the traffic demands of an intranet within the group. The fact that designers use Mac and the rest of the office uses PCs has to be borne in mind and a system that will work for both installed. We found nonsensical and counter-situations, which are detailed in the report section under 'E-mail' (page 168). The amount of time this can take, combined with the frustration that the whole scene engenders, is potentially very damaging to productivity, profitability and morale.

Remote working

One person in particular highlighted the problem that he had just been given a very heavy laptop, which meant that he could not travel light. As he travels all the time, this is a factor that needs to be taken into consideration. Like a lot of remote workers, he tends to develop his own systems and be a bit of a maverick. However, he admits only too readily that he also needs training on the use of preferred templates for the sales forecasts and other required data that he needs to be able to feed straight into the system from wherever he is.

Other people also identified these heavy computer problems. Laptops free up the people to work – from home, and travelling on business – without slowing down the functions needed to run the group.

Training

Throughout the group, a number of people identified that they needed some training to be able to use their computers effectively. There is a hugely positive feeling among people that the group could go far and they want to do their bit to help it along but are frustrated by their own perceptions of having to learn on the hoof rather than being able to learn at a deeper level. Obviously a balance needs to be drawn here but making these willing and enthusiastic people feel better about their skills and improvements would pay back time and again to the group.

As more systems are implemented, this training need must be factored in for the office to function properly. This could take the form of one-to-one personal training as well as help files and suggestions placed on the intranet.

The Main Report

Now to the main body of the report, which gives specific details for the board to consider; first on the most customer-facing aspects of your business.

Websites

Currently the group has two websites available to the public. One is a group website, while the other is specifically for the product line with its UK audience. Each site is looked at individually.

The company has not, to date, taken advantage of the Internet in any of the realms of e-commerce or any form of electronic business to enable current revenue streams to be more automated or to develop new ones.

We understand that one subsidiary is 'quite a long way down the line' in commissioning its own website, which will include e-commerce. However, no discussion on this project was forthcoming. We think this may be a protective stance by a newly taken-over CEO – but this will cause problems with consistency of branding if not addressed as part of the rest of the takeover. We are also not yet privy to the details of the takeover and the timescales for assimilation of name and brands, if desired.

We believe that the present group website is potentially damaging to the group (and its posture in developing into a more inter-nationally recognised company) because the way the site has been created is not only technically incompetent, but suffers badly from poorly targeted, mixed, confused and incomplete messages. In short, it's a communications nightmare.

It is urgent that this be addressed if the organisation is to be taken seriously as a company that understands the dimension and usage of Internet technologies and the World Wide Web.

The knotty question of domain names and branding needs to be reviewed urgently – not least the problem that already exists with another company 'parking' on the .co.uk version of your group name. When we first started researching your group we tried the obvious UK focused domain name of www.[Group].co.uk – only to find a company trading in a totally different arena but named the same apart from the words 'of companies' being inserted between the word 'Group' and 'plc'. (We immediately alerted the chairman to this conflict; he was previously unaware of it.) In principle the domain name endings .org, .com, .biz, .net and .co.uk should all be registered for each brand as it comes up so that routing to the principal site of all traffic can be effected.

When registering domain names in future, it is essential to bear in mind the different routes that your intended audiences are likely to follow and to be one step ahead of them by registering the appropriate domains in your own name and rerouting to the principal site. It is quite straightforward to register domains in one batch now that there is so much usage of the Internet and more people are more familiar with the medium.

For branding reasons it may be appropriate to take this further and register brands in other national domains so as to protect and to capture the markets in these territories, as well as looking to .eu endings to cover Europe. There needs to be a debate as to whether this would make life easier by reducing the number of geographical nation states that need to be catered for.

A business process needs to be set up whereby, as soon as a new brand is in planning and prior to its being implemented, the appropriate domain names are immediately registered and recorded for renewal or deletion at a later date. Trademarking should also be looked into and set in train for all the geographical areas in which the group intends to trade both now and in the future.

The Group Corporate Website

The current site suffers from poor planning and focus as well as being technically incompetent. Partly this is as a result of there being no one within the group who has had much experience of working with web developers and editors before; but a large part of the 'blame' must go to the web design company for, apparently, not having asked some of the most basic questions about the need for the site before starting the design process.

We would recommend that going back to basics at this juncture will enable the site to fulfil the communications purposes for which it should originally have been set up and to benefit the group tremendously in the process.

General Points

- It does not appear that anyone has actually sat down with the designers to determine what the point of the site is, what messages are trying to be put across, who are the target audiences, what they would want to look for on a group site, what feedback you want from your visitors and what kind of an impression your visitors will go away with.

- In particular there has been no attempt at updating the site, leaving visitors with the impression that either nothing ever happens at the group, or that the company does not care about its on-line image.

- Navigation buttons need to be rethought to enable visitors to find what they want within three clicks – which is the business norm.

- Each page needs a 'hook' to give the visitor comfort that it will be worth their while visiting it.

- The 'Smarties'-type navigation buttons look good, but do not line up properly because of the way that the navigation bar has been constructed. This method of construction also means that when the menu changes colour – as it does for each of the separate areas of the site – the download times are increased, as new buttons need to be downloaded for each page.

Splash Page

- The opening (splash) page has a badly cropped graphic of the group logo and has poorly written JavaScript, meaning that when the 'mouse-over' instruction has ended, the instruction to 'Click here' remains on the status bar.

- It is unclear what the point of this splash screen is, in any case. Normally such pages are inserted as a 'filler' while other code downloads in the background. This is not the case on this site. In fact the page appears to have no communication or branding purpose.

Home Page (First Page after Splash Screen)

- Some words and image to hook the visitor should download fast, giving a flavour of the group and helping them focus on what the site is all about.

- The e-mail addresses and 'Contact us' details should be moved to a

'Contact us' page, which also should contain postal addresses, phone and fax numbers and have maps to download for visitors looking for each of the individual locations. Alternatively the contact details should appear in small font in a frame, visible on every page and remaining constant so that visitors do not have to spend a long time finding out how to get hold of the group.

- The potted history of the group should be moved to an 'About us' page and should be considerably expanded and include an organisation chart of the key players.
- On entering the site from the splash screen there are no fewer than 39 images that have to be downloaded – partly due to the fact that all the text appears to have been saved as .gif (i.e. graphics) files. This accounts for the very long loading times, and will almost certainly mean that you will lose visitors who do not want to wait to get into the site in this way. Saving text as .gif files is a very crude solution to a common problem in designing sites and is bound to cause your visitors problems, which is why most designers frown upon it. There are plenty of other workable solutions, which are in common use across the Internet.
- There are no 'meta tag' content words incorporated into the home page by which search engines would pick up the group site. However, they have been incorporated into the individual frames – the result of which is that individual frames would load from the search engines without any of the navigation frames needed to allow visitors to access other areas of the site. (This can easily be corrected in the coding.)
- The 'Smartie' button belonging to the home page is not the same colour as its navigation background, which is inconsistent with every other menu page.

Subsidiary 1 Franchising

- This page doesn't say enough. It is unclear whom it is aimed at.
- There is nothing to encourage potential customers to contact the group.
- The sub pages are so basic that they belie the flexibility of the web.

Subsidiary 2 Merchandising

- There is not enough information and it is boring.
- Who is it aimed at?
- What do they want to know?
- Why should anyone respond to it?

Subsidiary 3 Artwork

- Once again it is unclear what messages are trying to be delivered
- The poor visual quality of the product designs on the pages is because they were saved as .gif files instead of photo quality .jpgs This will act in a totally negative way toward people commissioning your artwork subsidiary for work.
- The text is bald and completely underplays the value of the connections and blue chip client base.
- There is no carrot to lead potential partners to try to work through the artwork subsidiary.
- The list of clients is unimpressive in its presentation although the names of the clients themselves are impressive.

Press

- This should actually be entitled 'cuttings' but instead it will draw journalists to an area that they would probably not be that interested in.
- These take an inordinately long time to download and in order to obviate this these pictures should have been 'optimised' for web loading. They have instead been saved by scanning in the cuttings and saving them as large .jpg (photo) files.
- If the cuttings *really* have to be saved as picture files it would be normal to save the text part of the picture (i.e. in two colours) as .gif files. In our tests using an ordinary 56 kbps modem, we found this simple expedient would have had the effect of reducing the download time by around 75%!
- There is no way anyone could find out what it is they are being asked to download until after they have downloaded it. And

worse, we understand that it is only envisaged that press cuttings are updated quarterly, when the ethos of the web would normally dictate that they should be updated at the very minimum on a weekly basis.

Group News

- This page is misnamed and should be aimed at the press, but journalists would be unable to find useful information. Normally they would expect to find past news releases, chronologically laid out, to which they could refer. The present layout neither gives journalists an opportunity to know what stories are there until they have looked, nor does it even give the dates of the news releases themselves!
- Product roll-outs and product news should be available on an obviously named page.
- Old news needs to be deleted, or made clear that it is old news in an archive file rather than news that is still up on site despite being well past its date.
- Page 5 of these 'news' pages is the only place we could find on the whole site with the corporate address in it. However, the e-mail address given is wrong.
- The .jpgs of the products have not been optimised, leading to very slow downloads. In our tests we were able to reduce the download times by around 80% simply by optimising the graphics.
- The references to page numbers give no clue to the visitor as to what they'll find if they click on them. This is totally at odds with the ethos of the web and it would be better to give a proper reference to draw the visitor through.

Financial News

- The message that is most easily acquired from the site is that the group share price has been falling – which is not what we believe should be the main message given out!
- The year reads '192000'. The JavaScript routine has been wrongly coded.

- The opening paragraph 'BRINGING YOU THE LATEST MARKET SHARE PRICES' together with the live clock implies that the share price shown really is the latest price. It is only further down the page that you find that it is not up-to-date. (Incidentally, putting words in CAPITAL LETTERS on a web page is equivalent to SHOUTING!)
- The half-yearly report to 30 October does not have an issue or publication date although the last paragraph talks of an offer of a free copy if ordered within 14 days. 14 days of when?

The Product Website

Many of the problems to do with the group website are reflected in the construction of the product site. Following discussions, we put together a list of questions framed for the group to put to the current web developers as well as some contractual questions following on from the letter from their agents dated 15 November 1999.

All these questions were formulated in a non-technical – and in some cases in a seemingly naïve – manner in order to achieve the answers without spoiling the relationship. We have not seen any answers to the latter but include some of the answers from the web developers.

Knowledge Management and Communications

A communications and business audit combined with an Internet audit would not be complete without considering how Internet technologies could be used internally to benefit an organisation.

In interviewing the key players we consistently found frustrations with internal communications across the entire group. Many of these could be addressed by the provision of an intranet – that is, an internal Internet. But basically the real problems are that people do not communicate because of a culture of secrecy, which is dictated by how the board runs itself.

Head Office

We interviewed 22 key individuals identified by the board, including: chairman, CEO, FD, commercial director, business development director, legal director, company secretary.

Northern Office

We interviewed five key individuals identified by the board.

Scottish Artwork Office

We interviewed five key individuals identified by the board.

London

We interviewed five key individuals identified by the board.

Findings

In this audit we looked into all areas of the business, from the most basic messaging through to ready access of accounts and other need-to-know material and design work, from conception through to style guide and approval, so that our analysis and findings could be accurate and the most useful to the group.

Almost without exception your people identified poor internal communications as a barrier to working effectively. One senior manager went so far as to call it a 'communications breakdown'. Certainly from our observations in HQ, no one from any department or division seemed to have much of an idea what anyone else was doing – even within their own department. This is partly because the company is growing at such a phenomenal rate but it does need to be addressed if the company is not to trip over itself while it grows.

This was not apparent in Scotland, where as far as we could tell, there was excellent internal communication and the whole team worked together to common objectives. However, there were huge communications gaps between HQ and Scotland as well as between the other subsidiaries.

E-mail

HQ

We were surprised that in spite of the majority of key players having access to e-mail it appeared that this medium was not utilised for some internal communications. This might have been because the e-mail was only set up for dial-up e-mail, but no one internally appeared to have any idea how the system worked, calling in an out-sider only when the system broke down.

This resulted in, for instance, reception personnel running round delivering yellow stickies – with all the problems they can cause – for simple messaging rather than using e-mail. It was also pointed out that managers were unable to retrieve their e-mail when out of the building since they had no dial-up access to the server.

Some people have organised the reception of e-mail via personal Hotmail accounts but this creates an additional barrier to working easily as e-mails to the group then need to be forwarded to the personal Hotmail accounts by someone else. This carries with it the problems of audit trailing and filing. It also builds disinformation and malinformation – even if there is no intent to do so.

There is also the question of company law in that under UK law, a company is required to display its registration number and address on all correspondence. This has clearly not been incorporated into the use of e-mail within the Group. This can most easily be done by setting up an e-mail 'signature' which is automatically appended to the foot of every outgoing e-mail without further input from the author. The 'signature' facility can also be used to good effect for adding market-ing messages.

Scotland

The artwork subsidiary has a real problem with its e-mail due to the fact that – when we visited – there was no network of computers and there was only one machine connected to the Internet which itself had a broken floppy-disk drive. This meant that if anyone wanted to send or receive an e-mail, not only did they have to use one e-mail address for everyone, but also they had to save and deliver text from one machine to another using a 100 mb zip disk.

Because of these difficulties the e-mail tends to be used as little as possible thereby exacerbating already poor communications between Scotland and HQ.

We understood on our visit that authority had already been given for installation of an Ethernet network – initially linking the Mac machines – which could allow e-mail to be made available to all those using Macs.

London

The state of communications in the London office was very basic with many PCs lying around disconnected, and two machines both able to connect to one e-mail address, but without being able to differentiate which machine picked up which messages. At present, e-mails are printed out and given to the intended recipients, who then get the secretary to reply on their behalf.

Frustration was evident from the comment given by one of the people, who said that with her contacts she would normally have expected around 90% of her incoming and outgoing messages to be sent on e-mail, but because of the present system she estimated that figure was actually no more than 2%. It was 'too much of a hassle', she explained, to try to get it sorted out.

The frustration is even more evident downstairs where the franchising division has to get e-mails transcribed upstairs if at all. It was understood that 'someone' would eventually sort out an e-mail solution, but no information had been given as to when this might be.

The overall level of frustration in London is exacerbated by an almost total lack of IT support and integration of any systems whatsoever (see below).

Opportunities to Review How Things Work

With the enormous growth that the group has enjoyed in the last few years, combined with the mergers and acquisitions already achieved – and those that may already be in train – enabling fast and comfortable execution of normal office functions is essential. If nothing is done at this stage it is likely that office processes, which have grown in volume beyond that originally envisaged, will swamp the growth of the company.

We found messaging, common access to various items of information and basic communication on many day-to-day matters essential for the company are limping along and taking far longer than they need to. Throughout the group we came across numerous examples of how the provision of a basic intranet/extranet could save both time and money in the normal business process, as well as solve many of the problems caused by poor communications. As with all Internet communications media, an intranet can be given varying levels of security and access.

For example, if you identify the roles and functions played in a dynamic company the following are some of the things you could do with an intranet.

Accounts

An intranet would make it possible for accounts, spreadsheets and other need-to-know information to be available to specific people. The person wanting the information could – subject to status – access it in their own time simply by entering a password to get to the required data. This should be as easy for them to access when travelling (via the extranet) as it is in the office.

An up-to-date share price could also be displayed, if this was desirable, by incorporating a specific Internet page within the confines of the intranet. Sales forecasts could be 'posted' to the intranet from anywhere in the world to be available for the board and the Monday meetings.

Products

The present system – whereby some 50 to 60 sheets of style guides need to be printed off in runs of up to 500 at a time – could be scrapped in favour of having all such designs available for ready access on the intranet. Not only would this speed up the approval, sign-off and franchising procedures, making it possible for anyone to view the designs wherever they might be in the world, but it would also save the costs of printing off the style guides – which could be in the order of £30 000 per year – and even make them available to third parties such as franchisees.

An added benefit would be that all subsidiaries could be included in the design loop at a much earlier stage than they are at present, obviating the need for redesigning and the costly delays of having to send hard copy via couriers. Project planning, progress of roll-outs and work under wraps should also be available for those who need to know and for further input.

There should be a section on the history and background of the various products. This would be useful for new members of staff to 'catch up' as well as providing a repository of approved information for occasions when it is demanded by outsiders.

Remote Working

There is a clear problem found in any remote working in getting clearances for designs and sales forecasts; for example, in the Monday meeting, delivering messages and co-ordinating diaries across the group. In the case of the franchising outpost in London, this involves parcels being regularly despatched and received by expensive carriers when the simple provision of a scanner and digital camera (costing no more than £350 in total), allowing pictures to be placed on the intranet, could drastically reduce the number of parcels needed to be sent, with a corresponding reduction in cost and time.

Human Resources

Many of the business needs for the people side of the business can be available without delay through an intranet. For instance:

- Holiday charts
- Template forms
- Staff handbook
- Induction information for new starters, such as the role of each company and each division
- Internal telephone numbers
- Useful phone numbers
- Group company backgrounds
- Organisational charts
- People and roles
- Addresses of companies within the group
- Maps of how to reach each company
- Recruitment

- Staff magazine and notices
- Internal e-mail
- Suggestion box

Marketing

It is important to have an effective internal marketing presence so that all staff are kept fully up-to-date with the messages that the company is putting out and its stance on various business issues. (For instance, there is nothing worse than staff being asked for information at an exhibition and not knowing what the public line of the company is.)

All news releases should be included – just as on the company website (and it is likely that the latter could simply be incorporated into the intranet). In addition, all press cuttings should be posted, since having public recognition is a great internal morale booster and also engenders curiosity as people continually update their knowledge.

Any advertising or TV campaign can also be posted – including a streaming video of TV adverts – as well as a schedule of screening times.

Reception

There are a number of practices used in Reception that have obviously stayed with the company since it was very small. Some of these are more time-consuming than they need be, as well as potentially inefficient, and they could lead to a poor image of the group. For instance, as already mentioned, telephone messages are taken on yellow 'Post-it' notes and subsequently hand-delivered to the appropriate recipient. There is a delay in the message getting to the recipient; and because of their nature they could easily get stuck on to something else and lost.

Reception has a serious problem in being able to identify callers to the main door, as there is no visual contact, and then in logging visitors in and out. This could easily be remedied with an inexpensive camera connected to the intranet, allowing anyone a view of the front door.

This idea could be taken further in helping with security around the building and also in the car park. Inexpensive cameras can be set up to deliver streaming video of any area where security could be a concern.

At present all post is opened in Reception and then logged in and out by hand into a loose-leaf log. We were not told what happened to this log, but if monitoring of all incoming post is really a necessity, anyone could determine if a particular item of mail had arrived for them by viewing such a log on the intranet.

General Information

With a company growing this fast, it is quite likely that general information will not reach everyone in the group. Changing the culture by posting information on the intranet and expecting people to look this up – and then inviting their comments – will engender a greater feeling of belonging and of being valued, and will enable the company to cope with the next stage of growth with the minimum number of hiccups.

This could be achieved by, for instance, posting a 'sanitised' resumé of the Monday morning meeting; and having a bulletin board, encouraging people to add their comments. This could also improve creativity.

Strategic Vision Using Internet Technologies

In looking at the way Internet technologies could deliver a series of faster, broader revenue streams and increased valuation – as well as improving time, energy and cash flow on existing ways of doing business – we have identified a number of key areas that could be implemented in the long and short term. This is on the premise that the goals are massive share price growth, mergers and acquisitions.

In the short term these would include the following areas:

- Listserv investor and City information to potential and existing investors
- Webcasting – both sound and vision
- Artwork

- Merchandising
- Marketing Information
- Database creation
- Adding suppliers and partners to an extranet

Listserv Investor and City Information

Listserv is an automated system that sends targeted e-mail to named individuals who have indicated that they want to receive the information, with no administrative costs beyond that of writing and checking the message. It is an ideal way for companies to maintain a relationship with their audiences without forever sending out large quantities of printed matter with all its attendant costs. Listserv also obviates the need for someone to input the recipients into a database since this is done automatically on receipt of the e-mail requests.

As the group has some 25 000 shareholders, using Listserv to supply those who have an Internet connection could save a considerable amount of postage and time. In addition a section of the group website (passworded if deemed necessary) could be devoted to shareholders, thus doing away with the need for a newsletter for all shareholders.

Conclusion

These extracts from communication audits give an indication of the kind of matters that can be addressed successfully.

T E N

Sounding Off

Communications in business is all about common sense and being practical. Most people think that they are good communicators but the truth is somewhat different. Inevitably the main reason for poor communication stems from the practice of 'opening mouth before deciding what to say' and letting all the words fall out in no structured way.

Without thinking clearly through your messages and the most appropriate means of imparting them, communications is doomed to failure.

Go back to basics and ask yourself these questions in relation to any intention to communicate:

- Why?
- How?
- When?
- To whom?

Effective communication can be almost guaranteed if realistic answers are given to these questions and you have a plan. Inevitably there will be external forces that try to shake you off the straight and narrow; but without a communications plan – ideally looking forward over the next 12 months in considerable detail as to what you are trying to achieve – there's little point in being merely reactive. It's all too easy to lurch from day to day without giving any direction to the business.

So, be clear about what you are trying to achieve and why. When you understand that, then the mechanics of it follow on. Whether you are talking about press relations or internal communications, whether you are using electronic vehicles or face-to-face, these are only tools.

The critical bit is understanding what it is you are trying to do and why. And then the tools become reasonably obvious.

Keep it simple and don't over-complicate. Don't get buried in jargon. That's why everybody thinks that doing communications or PR is easy. Everybody thinks that they can do it, but they can't necessarily. When it's done well it looks easy, but it isn't. Usually if you have done it well it's because you have done it simply.

Don't underestimate the power of communication. Good corporate communications are critical to business success.

Index